THE
SCIENCE
OF
HOCKEY
THE MATH, TECHNOLOGY, AND DATA BEHIND THE SPORT

KEVIN SNOW
FOREWORD BY JOHN VOGL

SPORTS PUBLISHING

Sports Publishing books may be purchased in bulk at special discounts for sales promotion, corporate gifts, fund-raising, or educational purposes. Special editions can also be created to specifications. For details, contact the Special Sales Department, Sports Publishing, 307 West 36th Street, 11th Floor, New York, NY 10018 or sportspubbooks@skyhorsepublishing.com.

Sports Publishing® is a registered trademark of Skyhorse Publishing, Inc.®, a Delaware corporation.

Visit our website at www.sportspubbooks.com.

10 9 8 7 6 5 4 3 2

Library of Congress Cataloging-in-Publication Data is available on file.

Cover design by David Ter-Avanesyan
Cover photo credit: Getty Images

ISBN: 978-1-68358-465-0
Ebook ISBN: 978-1-68358-466-7

Printed in the United States of America

This book is dedicated to my four favorite people in the world:
Mom & Dad
Christine & Alex
xxoo

CONTENTS

FOREWORD BY JOHN VOGL

In the early days of team website reporters, the goal was to stay out of the way. The writers would hang out in the back of interviews, let newspaper and TV reporters ask all the questions, then scoop up the quotes and post a story.

That never worked for Kevin Snow. He was too inquisitive.

A decade ago, Kevin transformed the Sabres' website from a ticket hub to a multimedia centerpiece. And he did it with his writing, his hockey knowledge, and his desire to get inside the game. While his team-employed cohorts around the NHL were content to piggyback, he wanted the whole hog.

Kevin would stand shoulder to shoulder with us reporters from "traditional" media and ask as many questions as we did. His specialty was follow-up questions. Often, the player or coach would give an answer that was perfectly suitable for a TV soundbite or newspaper notebook. Then Kevin would go deeper, asking the coach why he thought that or how the player acquired the skills and know-how to do what he did.

And in those instances, the script flipped. We were scooping up good quotes from the team website reporter rather than the other way around.

So while talking to Kevin as he conducted interviews for *The Science of Hockey*, it was no surprise to hear how long his chats went. He'd schedule thirty- to forty-five-minute talks with people in this book, but they'd regularly turn into hour-plus discussions. Kevin would hear something intriguing and ask the right follow-up, which would get folks talking more. And you'll benefit while reading.

A puck is vulcanized rubber, but it's also more than that. Every NHL arena has an ice surface, but what makes Edmonton so special and how do architects improve the view of that ice? Kevin dives into the physics of skating and the physical nature of hockey.

He does so with a worldwide view of the game after experiencing it across the globe.

I can still see us sitting alongside the river in Heidelberg, Germany, the chants of Adler Mannheim fans reverberating in our ears hours after a game. The Sabres had played an exhibition against the German league club, and it was unlike anything seen in North America. The legion of fans behind the net never sat down and never stopped chanting—not for one second.

Kevin has repeatedly taken Buffalo backers to a picturesque bay in Traverse City, Michigan, where the Sabres would play in a prospect tournament. Before Rasmus Ristolainen, Zemgus Girgensons, and Nikita Zadorov became NHL regulars, Sabres fans knew their stories because Kevin traveled to tell them.

His travels, of course, have included NHL cities and arenas. He's done interviews in the Madison Square Garden dressing room, walked the catwalk of Calgary's Saddledome, and been behind the scenes in Los Angeles as a busy arena transformed from a hockey palace to a basketball mecca in a matter of hours. He not only knows the game, but he also knows how much work goes into hosting and playing it. He's seen it from the inside of an organization. He's mingled in the front office and the locker room, talking to executives, players, and equipment managers to gain their unique insights.

As a lifelong hockey fan, Kevin is aware of how deep fandom runs. Games matter to people. But it's also still just a game, a pastime to be enjoyed. It's supposed to be fun. Few games were as much fun as the inaugural Winter Classic in Buffalo on New Year's Day 2008. The joy of being outside has become an annual tradition thanks to that snow globe contest between the Sabres and Penguins.

Kevin got the fun started before puck drop. In charge of the game notes, he created a "did you know" stat for the ages:

"The Sabres and Penguins both enter today's game with an all-time record of 0–0 when playing outdoors on a Tuesday afternoon in January."

Not surprisingly, the NHL selected him to manage a project that redesigned the league's media game notes. His humor shines through in his writing. His curiosity comes through in his questions. His knowledge is always on display. *The Science of Hockey* is further proof.

1

THE PUCK

Let's face it, the hockey puck isn't exactly the sexiest of the various sporting implements. At first glance, it's hard to get excited about a black slab of vulcanized rubber with knurled edges that measures three inches in diameter, one inch in thickness, and weighs six ounces.

But there is something magical about that piece of vulcanized rubber and the memories they have made over the years. For some, it was about the first time you played the game. For others, it's the first game you attended or the ones you've watched with friends.

For Ethan Prow, that memory was about fulfilling his lifelong dream.

When I made my way to KeyBank Center in Buffalo on December 29, 2021, I honestly wasn't expecting much. Making the playoffs was already out of the question for the Buffalo Sabres and New Jersey Devils, so it was really just an opportunity to enjoy a night out with a friend and watch some NHL hockey.

With injuries and COVID wreaking havoc on the Buffalo roster, the twenty-nine-year-old Prow was called up from the Sabres' taxi squad earlier in the day. After six seasons of toiling in the minor leagues—along with spending 2020–21 in the German league—Prow would finally make his NHL debut against the Devils that night.

Late in the third period with the Sabres trailing by two goals, Prow darted in from the point and buried the rebound from a Victor Olofsson shot behind Devils goaltender Mackenzie Blackwood. Prow had scored his first NHL goal, in his first NHL game, on his first NHL shot.

As is tradition, one of Prow's teammates immediately retrieved the milestone puck from the net and skated to the bench to hand it off to one of the Sabres' equipment staffers. The puck would then be labeled and ready for Prow to keep.

So there was Prow after the game in the traditional photo op. Still clad in his sweat-soaked gear, a beaming Prow held that milestone puck in his hand, with the words "1st NHL Goal" handwritten in black Sharpie on a piece of white hockey tape that stuck to the knurled edge of the puck.

Prow had finally created that unforgettable moment, and that black slab of vulcanized rubber was the greatest thing he'd ever seen.

THE KING OF PUCKS

Just about two hours east of Montreal, in Sherbrooke, Quebec, sits an old, sixty-seven thousand-square foot army barracks that is the global headquarters for Inglasco, the largest distributor of hockey pucks in North America.

The company was founded in 1976 by Denis Drolet, the son of Leopold Drolet, who started Sher-Wood Hockey. Inglasco was originally a die-cut fiberglass company that supplied Sher-Wood with the fiberglass they used to put on wooden hockey sticks at that time.

Sher-Wood Hockey would eventually purchase Inglasco to start focusing on the sports licensing business, specifically hockey pucks. By the mid '80s they had grown to become the NHL's official puck supplier to every team in the league, a relationship that is still in place today.

"It's really evolved into Inglasco being called the puck king of North America," says Anthony Fisher, Inglasco's COO and general manager. "Not only do we have the exclusive rights with the NHL, there's also the AHL and ECHL, along with partnerships with Hockey Canada and USA Hockey. We also have licensing agreements for other items such as water bottles, wall plaques, and mini sticks."

Inglasco produces more than five million pucks per year, and owns all the proprietary recipes and molds. All of the NHL game pucks are produced at Soucy Baron, a rubber products manufacturer in Saint-Jerome, Quebec, about a ninety-minute drive north of Montreal. The remainder of the novelty and other collector pucks are typically outsourced to a Slovakian manufacturer.

THREE STEPS TO GLORY

Just like there are three periods in a hockey game, prepping an official game puck for action now involves three steps thanks to the NHL's puck tracking software that was launched in January 2021.

Every puck used in an NHL game gets its start at the Soucy Baron production facilities. Soucy Baron produces more than four hundred thousand pucks each year, with the ability to churn out thirty thousand per week at their peak.

"It's very much like a cake recipe," says Roch Gaudreau, Director of Method and Quality for Soucy Baron. "There are fifteen to twenty different ingredients in the compound itself, with each ingredient serving a different purpose."

However, unlike your great-grandmother's famous cake recipe that has been passed down through generations, Gaudreau isn't about to share any of the ingredients that make up this completely inedible delight. The only item he would divulge is the presence of carbon black, providing the puck with its trademark color. Pucks can be made in other colors, but without the carbon black it doesn't contain the same properties of the official NHL puck.

"There's really a misconception that a hockey puck is just whatever rubber packed into the shape. We often get calls from people that want to sell their used tires so we can make pucks for them," Fisher says. "They have no idea about the science that goes into the resins and the compounds, along with the carbon blacks and everything else to make the different qualities and types of products. It's really quite a process."

Once all the ingredients are checked for quality, they are released for preparation. This involves an employee following the recipe and weighing each of the materials to prepare them for the next step in the mixing process.

Soucy Baron has the capability to make a sixty-kilogram (132-pound) batch of compound in house, but they can also outsource to their sister company, Soucy Techno, if they need batches as large as 220 kilograms (485 pounds).

To prepare a sixty-kilogram batch, it takes about five to eight minutes to collect of all the ingredients. There are about ten to twelve pre-mixed ingredients, and at the station where the mixing is done, two or three other ingredients are weighed and inserted within the process.

Once added to the internal mixer, it typically takes about eight to ten minutes for everything to combine properly.

The final mixing process takes place in an external mixer, with the material added to a pair of cylinders that are not turning at the same speed, with a shear in between.

"This will do the dispersion, where you want all the ingredients to be evenly distributed within the raw material," Gaudreau explains. "Then you get some rubber slabs of raw material. If you are stretching them they will not go back to the original. This is a soft rubber, it's not cured. This is a raw material compound."

The puck begins to take shape in the compression mold. With a compression mold, the compound is prepared before the rubber blank is shaped freeform with a certain weight and geometry. The rubber blank is inserted into a cylinder about twenty-four inches long by eight inches in diameter. As it compresses, it will move itself around the cavity and start taking the desired shape.

Gaudreau points out that in the rubber industry, you always need to plan for an overflow of material that will eventually need to be trimmed. This is unlike plastic, where you don't need that because use you inject that temperature and the skin will build itself and it will not go through the cracks because the material will only change from a certain shape to shape. Because there is vulcanization with rubber material, there's a chemical change between the raw material and finished parts. This change is permitted with the pressure, the time, and the temperature.

The vulcanization of the puck takes place during compression. Vulcanized rubber is harder and non-sticky, and has a high tensile strength that is resistant to breakage under stress. Natural rubber is soft and sticky, with low tensile strength.

As the material is compressed, it is maintained and cured for fifteen minutes, using heat and sulfur to make it rigid and durable. Making sure the puck is fully cured is essential. Without enough time or enough pressure, there will be some porosity in the middle and this is a problem. The puck will not be flat, taking on a rounded shape, and the material will be kind of spongy.

Those two cylinders of rubber, which work out to be twelve pucks per cylinder, are put in a preformer. This machine will extrude the material and cut to the specific weight and geometry required for a puck. It's like a syringe, with a hydraulic platen pushing the material through an opening that is round in shape and matches the dimensions of a puck.

A finished puck is about 160 grams (.35 pounds) net weight, so ideally that blank or pre-shape will weigh around 175 grams. This will account for the extra material required in manufacturing rubber. You want to be able to fill the cavity and have a small amount of material flowing out to ensure you have all the cavities full.

When you cure that blank, you will push on the raw material, it will fill the entire cavity and the overflow will come just in between all of the top plates. When you extract the puck you will take all that excess material you put in the garbage, removing the ten to fifteen grams from the puck.

Most of the operation is done by hand, except at the end. When the pucks are coming out of the tool, there will be a small amount of rubber that still will not do a net shape of the cylinder of the hockey puck. On both the top and bottom of the puck there's a line there and there will be an excess of rubber that will not be net fit. The puck is then placed in a deburring machine that will turn automatically, reshaping those two sides.

The puck's knurled edge also takes shape during this process. This crosshatched diamond pattern rings the outside edge of the puck, allowing for better control during play.

As expected, there's a strict quality control process that the pucks are put through before being shipped. A select number of pucks from each batch are checked for their weight, dimensions, and thickness. In addition, they test the resilience at zero degrees Celsius, along with the hardness at both room temperature and zero degrees Celsius. A certificate of analysis accompanies each batch when shipped.

According to the *Boston Globe*, once the pucks are deemed game ready by Soucy Baron officials, they are sent to SMT, Inc., (SportsMedia Technology) in Raleigh, North Carolina. It is here where the NHL's high-tech puck tracking software is inserted into the puck, including a battery, circuit board, and light tubes. The infrared light beam emitted from the puck works in tandem with a series of cameras and sensors that have been installed in all thirty-two arenas to collect a variety of data in regards to game play.

THE FINISHING TOUCH

The last stop for the puck is at Inglasco's high-tech printing facility to apply the logos for each team on one side of the puck, and the official NHL insignia on the other side. As Fisher explains, this isn't just about slapping a logo on a puck. A lot of time and money has gone into developing the printing process.

"We have a number of different silkscreen printers that have specifically been designed and manufactured for pucks. These are proprietary and were designed exactly for this purpose. We have the ability to print eight colors, six colors, or three colors. There's no other printers like this in the world."

A new twist was added to the silk-screening process for the Winter Classic in 2019 in order to help out referees and provide the best playing conditions possible.

A thermochromic coating, created by PPG Paints, was added to the side of the puck that features the NHL logo. This coating is applied over that logo and will turn purple when the puck is adequately frozen for game play. During play, the pucks are stored in a cooler inside the penalty box area to maintain their ideal temperature of approximately fourteen degrees Fahrenheit.

According to Fisher, the shelf life of a playable puck is between ninety seconds to two minutes. That's about the time when the puck performance will start to decline, resulting in additional bouncing and rolling. As the puck warms up, the coating turns grey, a signal to the referee that the puck needs to be removed from the game.

If this process sounds familiar, then you are someone that enjoys your beer. This is the same thermochromic technology introduced by Coors Light in 2007 to turn the mountains blue on their beer cans that were at their optimal drinking temperature. Put this piece of trivia in your back pocket and drop some knowledge on your friends the next time you've gathered to watch a game and crush a few cold ones.

HOW WE GOT HERE

Long before the days of vulcanized rubber, various items were used to play the game of hockey. Dating back to the 1800s, legend has it that frozen cow dung was used to play the earliest forms of outdoor hockey. I, for one, sure wouldn't want to have been on the ice when that puck started to warm up a bit!

Rubber balls used to play lacrosse were also a popular item later in the century. The balls would be cut in thirds and the middle section would be used as the puck, a precursor to the style and shape we see today. But as the game grew in popularity, using this method became very impractical because they couldn't keep up with the demand.

Believe it or not, the first truly flat pucks were square blocks made of wood. The first recorded indoor game of hockey took place in Montreal in 1875. But instead of using the rubber version for that game, they opted for wood as a safety precaution. There were concerns that the rubber version could easily be propelled into the spectators and cause injury, while the wood option would simply slide along the ice without the chance of being elevated.

The early 1900s introduced the practice of gluing pieces of tire rubber together to create what they thought would be a more durable puck. What sounded good in theory didn't seem to work very well, as the pucks regularly became unglued and split into pieces when struck by a stick.

The version of the puck we see today took its form in 1918, and hockey fans around the world have Art Ross to thank for that.

To many, Ross is most widely recognized for the Art Ross Trophy, the annual award presented to the NHL's leading scorer during the regular season. (Ross donated the trophy to the NHL in 1947.) But Ross was also a well-known player and coach, and most importantly, an innovator in the game of hockey.

During his 13-year playing career from 1905 to 1918, Ross is credited for being the first defenseman to rush the puck up the ice. While coaching the Boston Bruins in 1931, Ross became the first coach in NHL history to ever pull his goalie for an extra attacker in a game against the Montreal Canadiens.

Always looking to improve the game, Ross designed a new form of goalie net that the NHL adopted for use in 1927–28. Ross created a net with a B-shaped structure on top that was designed to catch pucks better and prevent dangerous rebounds. The NHL used this until 1984 when they switched to a modified version of Ross's original design.

Ross also designed a puck that the NHL started using in 1918. But it wasn't until 1940 when Ross was finally awarded a US patent for his design of the hockey puck.

Ross had removed the flat edges of the puck, replacing them with a beveled edge that prevented bouncing. More importantly, the updated version of Ross's puck was made from synthetic rubber developed during World War II, not the natural version. Ross had also molded a checkered pattern on the outside edge of the puck to make it easier to control. Known as the Ross-Tyer puck, it was the official puck of the NHL from 1942 to 1968.

Inducted into the Hockey Hall of Fame in 1949 and Canadian Sports Hall of Fame in 1975, Ross passed away at age seventy-nine in 1964.

Yet his beveled puck and knurled edges live on today.

FOX TRAX

When Fox Sports landed the national rights to air NHL games in the United States back in 1995, they wanted to do everything in their power to make the game more accessible. They forked over a $155 million rights fee (31 million dollars per year for five years), and the NHL was thrilled to have a partner that was committed to airing their product south of the border.

But Fox didn't want to just settle for the game rights; they wanted to do something monumental.

A common complaint among casual hockey fans in the US was that because of the speed of the game, they had trouble following the puck during the action. Armed with this knowledge, Fox Sports president David Hill came up with the idea for a color-enhanced glowing puck, believing it would magically broaden the audience for viewers who couldn't keep up with the black puck on the white ice.

Fox News CEO Rupert Murdoch loved the idea and immediately greenlighted a two million dollar R&D project.

Utilizing technology within a hockey puck turned out to be no simple feat. Not to mention this was 1995, and broadcast capabilities were nothing like they are today. Making it more difficult was the quick turnaround time, as it was set to debut months later at the 1996 NHL All-Star Game in Boston.

A system was devised wherein infrared technology would track LED lights that were embedded inside the puck with a battery and circuit board. The puck was literally sliced lengthwise like a bagel to get the devices inside, and then glued back together.

In order to track the puck's movements, special game cameras were designed that measured zoom, pan, and tilt. Additional sensors were placed throughout the arena to follow the puck in real time regardless of anything that may obstruct it.

Prior to the All-Star Game, a Fox Sports promo video hyped it as "the biggest technological breakthrough in the history of sports." (Excuse me? Instant replay would like a word with you.)

Despite some concerns during the late stages of testing, the puck was glitch-free during its All-Star Game debut. In video game-like fashion, a blue glow was superimposed over the puck as it moved across the ice. When it was shot, the puck emitted a blue tail akin to a streaking comet. That tail would be red if the puck exceeded a certain speed.

Fox deemed the puck a success, but it wasn't without its critics. Passionate hockey fans on both sides of the border weren't impressed with the kitschy puck, accusing Fox of putting ratings over the sanctity of the game.

There were even some detractors among the players, complaining that the doctored-up puck created performance issues because of its funky construction and modified weight.

Just like Fox's national NHL coverage, the glowing puck faded into broadcast oblivion at the conclusion of the 1998–99 season. But it hasn't been forgotten.

In 2012, Evan Winiker wrote in *The Huffington Post*: "The glut of question marks that shroud the glow puck's existence are bountiful, though one thing is certain, it will go down as the worst broadcasting innovation of our time."

SAFETY NET

Having spent many nights sitting in the end zone blue seats at Toronto's legendary Maple Leaf Gardens as a teenager, I can't tell you how many times I would cringe as a defenseman teed up a point shot that could easily get tipped and come flying my way. The thought of having netting there to protect me had never even crossed my mind.

Tragically, that all changed in 2002.

On March 16, 2002, thirteen-year-old Brittanie Cecil was in attendance at Nationwide Arena in Columbus, Ohio, to watch her hometown Blue Jackets take on Calgary. To make the night more special, the tickets were a gift from Brittanie's father for her birthday.

Midway through the second period, Cecil was hit by a puck that had been deflected into the stands. A shot from Columbus forward Espen Knutsen had been redirected off the stick of Calgary defenseman Derek Morris, striking Cecil in the left temple.

The game carried on without pause, and remarkably Cecil was able to walk to a first aid booth in the arena with only a visible cut on her forehead. She was transported to Columbus Children's Hospital in an ambulance as a precaution, and was admitted after suffering a seizure.

Cecil appeared to be turning the corner the next day, but a torn vertebral artery went undetected in a CT scan, ultimately resulting in severe clotting and swelling in her brain. Cecil would succumb to her injuries on March 18, just two days before her fourteenth birthday. It remains the only fan fatality in NHL history.

A lawsuit with the NHL was settled out of court in April 2004, awarding Cecil's family $1.2 million. Her legacy lives on with the Brittanie Nichole Cecil Memorial Scholarship Fund, but there's hope that some good came from that tragedy.

In June of 2002, the NHL ordered all arenas to install netting that would protect fans in vulnerable seating areas from pucks that could leave the playing surface. It was installed above the glass that borders the corners and end zones of each arena. In addition to the netting, the league also mandated that the protective glass that bordered the rink along the side boards had to be at least five feet high.

PUCK DYNAMICS

One of the benefits of watching hockey in high definition is the ability to see every twist and turn of a puck in a slow-motion replay. Not only does a shot rise and fall, but the change of direction can happen with the simplest and most subtle of touches.

It's just like seeing a pitcher in baseball manipulate the ball with his grip, and watching the spin of the laces as he changes the speed and trajectory of his pitch.

What these objects both have in common is the presence of air. As the puck is in the air, it's going to fly like a projectile so it doesn't go straight, but rather curves back toward the earth. A puck or ball in flight follows a parabolic path once it's put into ballistic motion, so it falls toward the earth.

"You have a parabolic trajectory when there's more air. In the case of the puck, air is important. It's actually kind of like the wing of an airplane. It's being airborne by the air, if it's tilted slightly upwards," explains Alain Haché, a professor in the physics department at the University of Moncton (New Brunswick). "If you look at a slow-motion shot from the blue line, often you'll see the puck travel at the same height the entire time. That would not happen if there wasn't any air, because of the aerodynamics of the puck.

"In order for that to work, the puck has to spin unto itself, like a frisbee. Because if the puck doesn't spin, you lose the ability for the puck to be oriented the same way."

To mix in another sports analogy, Haché compares this to a quarterback throwing a football. As the ball is released, the wrist motion creates a spin to give the ball added stability as it goes downfield.

It's this spin motion that's added by a shooter, quarterback, or pitcher that imparts a little bit of gyroscopic stability to the object being delivered.

In the case of hockey, it's how the shooter utilizes the stick that can dictate the path of the puck. The flex of the stick and the curve on the blade will both come into play, but ultimately it's the hand motion of the person making the pass or taking the shot that will determine how accurate the final outcome will be.

This is also where the knurled edging of the puck comes into play. Combined with the friction created by the presence of tape on the blade, a player is able to create the spin and accuracy required with each pass or shot.

"It's very critical in hockey. When they shoot the puck, especially with a wrist shot, they give it a flick with the wrist to make it spin so that it has a much more stable trajectory. If they don't impart that spin, you'll see the puck flickering in the air," Haché says.

"It's the same process for a saucer pass. You want a clean trajectory and easy reception. The puck is spinning unto itself, going up a bit in the air and then falling flat on the ice. If you have a player that can't do that, the puck will flip backwards on to itself and that's not very clean. It's difficult to catch a puck like that."

2

THE RINK

There was a stoppage in play midway through the first period of Game 1 of the Western Conference first-round series between Edmonton and Los Angeles in the 2022 Stanley Cup playoffs. As play was going to resume with an upcoming faceoff, one of the linesmen began tending to a rut in the ice. After trying to smooth it over with water and ice shavings, the Rogers Place ice crew was called out to take a look.

With a national TV audience watching across North America, Matt Messer, the manager of engineering and ice operations for Oilers Entertainment Group, suddenly became the most nervous person in the building.

Messer has been with the Oilers since Rogers Place opened in 2016, and he's turned the building into one of the league's gold standards when it comes to playing surfaces.

Rogers Place finished in second place in the NHLPA 2021–22 Player Poll, garnering 13.7 percent of the votes for having the best ice in the league. Montreal's Bell Centre was the leading vote getter for the fourth time at 39.6 percent.

This recognition from across the league wasn't lost on Messer.

"For me personally, that honor was huge. It's one thing when your home team players tell you how much they like the ice surface. I guess I get desensitized to it. But to have guys from the Eastern teams that only come here once a year say the same thing, it really means quite a bit to me and the entire crew."

Canada Life Centre (Winnipeg, 12.2 percent), T-Mobile Arena (Las Vegas, 5.8 percent), Xcel Energy Center (Minnesota, 2.8 percent), and Madison Square Garden (New York Rangers, 2.8 percent) rounded out the top six vote-getters.

Now in his tenth season of making ice at the NHL level (six with Edmonton, four in Calgary), Messer was kind enough to walk me through the process of how he preps the building for ice making, and what his normal maintenance routine is throughout the season.

INSTALLATION

It takes almost a week to get the ice into its game-ready state before the season begins, but Messer explains that the first few days of the process can often be the most crucial.

"Ideally, you're doing around six days to get it completed. That's just to make sure that you're doing everything properly, taking it nice and slow and not skipping any important steps," explains Messer. "And the most important step of that is the first day and that's cleaning the slab."

Cleaning the concrete floor may sound like a basic step, but if not done properly it can have long-term implications. The idea is to remove any dirt or contaminants, especially any oil that may have collected on the floor during the summer months. In large multi-use buildings like Rogers Place, there are usually concerts and other events that take place in the summer months. That means there has been alcohol spilled on the floor and various trucks and lifts that may have been out on the floor to work on things above the surface. All those contaminants can get into the concrete and they can actually absorb a little bit.

"If there are contaminants, the water will push away and it won't freeze properly," says Messer. "It's hard to describe, but it'll look kind of like a void area, like putting cooking oil and water together."

To rid the floor of any dirt and oils, Messer and his crew will use a floor scrubber and a special floor cleaner and an ultra-hot water wash. In the areas that can't be reached by the scrubber, they'll use hand mops to make sure nothing is left untouched. This process is repeated multiple times before Messer is confident they can start the ice-making process.

In order to cool the floor, brine water is pumped through the maze of steel pipes embedded in the concrete below to cool the slab. Brine water has a lower freezing point than water, so this prevents the solution in the pipes from freezing while getting the floor to its ideal temperature.

Using his ice plant control system, Messer will drive down the floor temperature to fourteen degrees Fahrenheit. He also prefers to add a couple of temperature sensors that are taped to the floor "just as a redundancy" to make sure the entire floor is properly cooled.

Once the floor is cooled, it's time to apply the sealing coats of water. This is normally just two to three very fine layers of water applied with a boom sprayer and a hose. This process ensures the entire concrete surface has a very thin layer of water over it and there are no gaps.

Unlike the normal backyard rink enthusiasts, Messer isn't just using tap water to make his ice. Rogers Place has its own water filtration system that produces reverse osmosis water that's already softened.

"Every building is different, but we can control how many total dissolved solids (TDS) we want in it," he explains. "When I worked for the Calgary Flames, we ran it at 100 TDS. Here we like to be around eighty TDS. The Edmonton city water is about 250 parts per million of TDS, so we filter out all the contaminants to get it down to about eighty."

According to Messer, you have to leave a little bit in because completely pure ice has a tough time bonding together. If a player is taking a hard turn at twenty miles per hour, you don't want that ice to explode and break away when he cuts hard into it. With hockey, you've got heavy players that are skating hard into the corners and you want that ice leveled up and not chipping away. Using water with lower TDS will offer a little more glide. But with the nature of hockey, it's preferable to run that TDS higher because it gives more grip.

The next step in the process is giving the ice its vibrant white look, and that comes in the form of Jet Ice Super White 3000 paint. Specially formulated for the ice making industry, Jet Ice is a biodegradable, clay-based powder that is mixed with water. Unlike a latex or oil-based paint, this paint is specifically designed to bond with water and freeze almost instantly.

Application of the paint varies from rink to rink. Messer prefers to use a cart-mounted system with a spray boom attached to the hose. It's typically a two-man operation with one guy running the spray boom, and the other guy pulling the hose.

If you've ever painted a wall, you know it's not ideal to apply the paint in multiple directions. That's pretty much the opposite of how Messer goes about his work.

"I usually do what's called a crosshatching on the third coat. We'll do the first two coats lengthwise down rink like everyone imagines. For the third coat we'll actually go side to side. The last coat will go up and down the rink again, just to make sure that we've got good coverage and we're not missing anything."

Some people marvel at the sight of a clean sheet of ice prior to a game or practice. But having seen the "raw" vibrancy of white, painted ice before it is sealed, it is visually stunning. When people have asked me what it compares to, my only thoughts are a freshly cut baseball field or the crisp green fairways at Augusta National.

Sealing the white ice comes next, and that's one of the most important steps in the process. After purging the paint from hose lines, a couple of very light coats of water are applied. If too much water is added too quickly, there's a possibility of the paint visibly floating on top of the water. When it's sealed perfectly, the ice is very shiny and glossy. But if there's paint there, you'll see a dull, white spot.

"It's very important that we move a little faster when sealing the first few layers after the white. We might angle the boom sprayer up a little bit; some guys like to carry it on their shoulder for the first few laps," explains Messer. "We'll probably make three to four more passes just to make sure everything's sealed, while looking for any trouble spots along the way. If all goes well, then we're ready to start putting down the logos and painting the lines."

PAINTING TIME

Getting the ice into game condition also involves adding all the lines and faceoff circles to their respective positions on the ice. There are eight faceoff dots on a rink, and Messer's crew utilizes each of these red markings as their way of prepping the entire surface. Instead of waiting until the ice is sealed, they will measure the dot locations out ahead of time, freezing a 5/16-inch nut in the center of the spot as a reference point. Messer figures that by doing this in advance, it saves his crew at least ninety minutes during the painting process. Otherwise they'd have to do all the measurements based off center ice and work their way backwards.

When it comes time to paint, almost everything is done by hand in Edmonton, courtesy of three aptly named Jet Ice colors: red line, blue line, and goal crease (blue). Not exactly the most creative names, but they get the job done. Might I suggest spicing things up with offside challenge blue and goaltender interference blue? Just a thought.

The only things not painted by hand at Rogers Place are the center ice red line, and the various team and sponsor logos positioned in various locations throughout the ice surface. Each of those are also created by Jet Ice using state-of-the-art large format digital printers, produced on reusable fabric that is placed directly on the ice.

ICE READINESS

When Messer's work is complete, the ice at Rogers Place will normally be about 1.5 inches thick. With a Western Hockey League junior team also calling Rogers Place home, Messer prefers to keep the ice a bit thicker because of the heavy workload the ice surface receives from hosting two teams.

There is no NHL standard for ice thickness, and Messer says it really varies from building to building, depending on its usage.

"Calgary also has a junior team at the Saddledome, and they typically run their ice around 1.25 inches. You definitely don't want to go anywhere near below an inch in any building because then it can become a danger area. Over the course of a game it gets ground down in certain spots, and the last thing we want is a player going at full speed and they hit concrete or a logo with their skate. It's really just a safety thing."

GAME-DAY ROUTINE

Keeping the ice in game condition is imperative for Messer and his crew, so they've developed a game-day routine that has been very successful for them.

With each team typically having some form of a thirty- to forty-minute morning skate, they will resurface the ice both before and after both teams are finished. As the Zamboni gently scrapes the ice, a layer of heated water is dispensed from the rear of the machine to fill any grooves and smooth out the top layer.

From there, they will flood the ice surface once per hour leading up to game time. As expected, there's a very scientific reason for Messer's meticulous care.

"The idea behind that is because when people ask me about ice, I explain to them that ice is kind of like a living thing. It's always kind of reacting to different environments. So if it's dry one day, I react differently to if it's very humid. So for lack of a better term, the ice gets thirsty.

"If you leave it for a long time, it's going to develop top layers that will get dry and brittle. By flooding every hour, we ensure that there's moisture going back into the ice, ideally keeping it in the optimal condition."

Food for thought the next time you grab some ice from the freezer, and the frozen cubes have become shriveled and brittle pieces of ice.

TEMPERATURE CHECK

Determining the ideal ice temperature for each building is dependent on the sports and the arena environment. Messer aims for a surface temperature of sixteen to eighteen degrees Fahrenheit at Rogers Place for Oilers games. Not only does that offer a very good base surface that holds up based on their water quality, it also creates good quality snow that won't impact the game negatively.

Messer will bump up the temperature during practices because warmer ice tends to get less damaged. With the repetition of doing practice drills in the same spots on the ice, the warmer ice won't break down as much. The one complaint that Messer gets from players with the warmer practice ice is that it feels "very grippy" on their skates.

With so many different competitions and performances taking place in arenas throughout the year, Messer needs to be cognizant of how the ice quality can affect the outcome of each particular event.

"Using the control system in our ice plant, we can designate what temperature we want to keep it at for each event. If we have a figure skating show where they're doing a lot of jumps, we'll actually raise that temperature to maybe twenty-four or twenty-five degrees Fahrenheit. They usually want the surface softer so they get more grip and there's fewer blowouts when they land.

"But if we were doing a short track speed skating competition here, we would want to bring that temperature down to fourteen degrees Fahrenheit because they want a lot more glide from the ice to increase their speed."

HOME ICE ADVANTAGE

There's more to a hockey arena than just a place for you to sit and watch the game being played on the ice. Over the years, these buildings have become palatial, multiuse facilities that are vital anchor points for community development and economic renaissance.

One of the shining examples of this is the District Detroit, the downtown home of the Motor City's four major sports teams.

Little Caesars Arena was the latest sports venue to become part of the district when it opened in 2017 as the home arena for both the Red Wings and the NBA's Pistons. The Detroit Tigers play their home games at Comerica Park, and right across the street you'll find Ford Field where the NFL's Lions call home. In addition, the historic Fox Theater is just a slap shot away from the arena.

The growth of the district also coincided with the rebirth of downtown Detroit, adding retail and restaurant options to several mixed-use neighborhoods, along with residential properties. Transportation even got an upgrade with the launch of the QLINE in 2017, a streetcar service that runs through the heart of the district, servicing both residents daily and tourists attending events at the three sports venues.

What makes Little Caesars Arena special is that it's more than just a place where sports are played. There are four dining and shopping locations that are open daily, and it also boasts office space for both the Red Wings and Google.

As a senior project manager with HOK, one of the leading architects for sporting venues around the world, Scott Ralston understands how important it is now for an arena to become an integral part of the community on a daily basis.

"These buildings are asked to do a lot. It's not just a hockey rink. That may be a singular focus for some people involved in that project. But we know as architects, we go all over the world and create venues like this. We have to create a venue that's good for community. If it's not good for community, it hurts cities. We always think of these as more than just a hockey rink."

JUST THE FACTS

Madison Square Garden in New York has the distinction of being the oldest arena in the NHL at fifty-five years old. Built in 1968, the iconic exterior of "The World's Most Famous Arena" remains the same, but the building's interior underwent major renovations from 2010 to 2013 to create a new arena bowl and concourses.

Opened in 1983 in advance of playing host to the 1988 Winter Olympics, the Scotiabank Saddledome in Calgary is the league's second oldest arena. Following close behind are SAP Center (San Jose, 1993), Honda Center (Anaheim, 1993), United Center (Chicago, 1994), and Enterprise Center (St. Louis, 1994).

There was a major arena construction boom in the late 1990s as fourteen current arenas were opened between 1996 and 2000. The most popular year to unveil a new building was 1996 when Tampa Bay, Nashville, Buffalo, Ottawa, Philadelphia, and Montreal all became new homeowners.

While UBS Arena (Elmont, New York) and Climate Pledge Arena (Seattle) both debuted in the 2021–22 season, the home of the New York Islanders is the NHL's shiniest new arena. With all construction projects in New York delayed during the beginning of the pandemic, the Islanders were forced to open the season with thirteen straight games on the road.

The first game at UBS Arena (located at Belmont Park) took place on November 20, 2021, resulting in a loss to Calgary. However, Islanders fans had no shortage of places to drown the sorrows that night when they discovered that their new arena boasts a whopping seventeen bars for them to congregate during games.

Similar to the MSG renovations, Climate Pledge Arena was redeveloped on the site of an existing structure formerly known as KeyArena that had been shuttered since 2018. The building had originally opened in 1962 to coincide with that year's World's Fair, and the original roof was incorporated into the construction of the renovated facility. The expansion Seattle Kraken played their first home game at Climate Pledge Arena on October 23, 2021.

In terms of capacity, Montreal's Bell Centre is the largest building in the NHL with room for 21,105 full-throated Habs fans. The smallest arena in the league is the Canada Life Centre in Winnipeg, although it definitely doesn't feel that way once you're inside. The "true north" Jets faithful easily make 15,321 fans sound like 25,000 in the league's most intimate setting.

The Jets may have their intimacy challenged if the Arizona Coyotes have their way. At the time of writing, the Coyotes were planning to start the 2022–23 season playing at Arizona State University's brand-new five thousand-seat arena. The team could stay as long as three years, as they try to somehow get a new multipurpose facility built in Tempe, Arizona, after spending the last eighteen years in Glendale. This entire situation has been embarrassing on all fronts, and remains the strangest hill for the NHL to die on. Relocation should've happened years ago to either Quebec City or Houston. But I digress.

ARENA TRENDS

With the newer facilities like Climate Pledge Arena, T-Mobile Arena (Las Vegas), and Rogers Place (Edmonton), the architects have taken advantage of evolving trends to go outside of the box with the design and construction. In addition to finding ways to incorporate them into the fabric of the community, they are now richer with amenities like lounges, standing room areas, and outside terraces. These not only enhance the spectator experience, but also they give the venue added value year round for things other than sporting events.

It's also about keeping up with the social element of a sporting event and how the building itself relates to the public realm. So many of the older arenas and event centers in North America are nothing more than windowless black boxes. Once you buy your ticket, the operator has you captured in their black box to consume their food and drink. And you do it because you have no other choice. Think of it as the circus rolling into town for three hours, and then packing up the tent and kicking you out when it's all over. Thanks for coming, please drive safely.

Today's buildings aren't being designed with the old-school traditional fan in mind. These are the passionate fans who will always spend $150 on a ticket, sit in their seat for three hours, eat some food, and go home when the game is over. Now it's more about the overall arena experience than it is the final score.

"All the things we're designing are just becoming more social. Younger people want to move around. They want to experience the building in different ways and hang out with their friends," explains senior architect Brad Clark of the design firm Populous, who played an integral role in the creation of T-Mobile Arena.

"Going back to the 1990s when I started in this business, I look back and realize we were missing the special sauce of what these buildings could really be. Back then, clients would ask for 100 suites and 1,200 club seats, and they were happy," Clark explains. "Now, there's just so much variety, and especially variety at different price points. Which I think is very critical because you have a bigger audience that's able to afford a premium experience. Whether that's a premium general ticket in the right place or an actual premium seat or club space."

DESIGN CHALLENGES

Clark and Ralston both agree that designing a hockey arena is more complex than most projects they encounter, mainly because of the multipurpose nature of the project.

It doesn't matter where the arena is; not only does it have to be a great venue for ice, but also it has to be a great venue for entertainment. The trend they're seeing is that entertainment in many ways is driving design decisions almost more than sports. Because there's so many events and so much revenue involved, it's not about just making it a world-class hockey venue for forty-one NHL home games. It's almost more important to be on the itinerary for the music artists on tour throughout the year.

"When you think about arenas, they are 100 percent enclosed buildings, and square footage and volume are always at a premium in terms of what a building is going to cost and how it's going to operate," Clark says. "The challenges we have are always going to be challenges of marrying the aspirations of client, community, and the fan base with the realities of budget."

The real challenge is finding the balance in all of that. That being the overall architecture of the building, and how you are able to design it to transition a seating configuration from an eighty-five by two hundred-foot ice rink, to a fifty by ninety-four-foot basketball court, to a center or end stage concert setting. These complexities will carry over to the mechanical systems and what the engineers will need to make it a successful hockey building. But that multipurpose nature just makes it harder for them as well.

And then there's the ice.

If people like Matt Messer are going to be able to do their job properly, the building has to be able to accommodate the various elements of the ice making process. Clark explains that from a mechanical standpoint, anytime that ice is involved it's going to be a highly customized system.

"We work with the best mechanical engineers in the world. Basically you end up customizing the systems to account for what is essentially the biggest enemy, which is humidity, in order to have the best ice. The challenge is reconciling those systems with the kind of complex architecture and structure that are involved in arena building.

"Active humidity controls, or desiccant systems are used—desiccants are materials that are really attracted to water, and water is attracted to them—to help pull the moisture out of the air. We're always going to have a desiccant system involved when we have ice."

The geographic location of the rink will also play a role in how to account for ice making during the design. What Messer has to deal with in a colder climate like Edmonton won't be the same as his counterparts in Vegas or Florida. Little things like where will the loading dock doors be in relation to the ice surface, and how much will they be open during the day can have an impact on ice quality.

In the design of T-Mobile Arena, Clark said, "We were fortunate in the way that the building needed to be oriented towards the Strip for the front door (main entrance), and that's east-facing. So when you get into the afternoon and evening hours, everything on that side of the building is shaded from the harsh desert sun."

Populous also opted for unique outdoor features in Las Vegas like balconies and terraces, along with more open concourse space, as opposed to the traditional vomitory fit seating bowl with dedicated passageways to each individual seating area. This style of design is more commonplace in baseball stadiums, but it is now being seen more and more inside arenas.

Even with nighttime events, the addition of these balconies and terraces definitely have the possibility of drawing in the warmer air from outside in a locale like Vegas. Clark says they worked closely with the design engineers to create an internal environment that wouldn't be affected by the heat and humidity of the Strip, and that included the installation of air curtains at all exterior openings.

If you're unfamiliar with an air curtain, they don't come with a rod and hooks. An air curtain creates an air seal by blowing a stream of air across a door or window opening. The biggest benefit of the air seal is that it separates environments while still allowing a smooth, uninterrupted flow of pedestrian traffic.

THE IDEAL RECIPE

When tasked with designing Rogers Place in Edmonton, Ralston drew on the experience he'd gained from an arena project completed nearly twenty years earlier. The hockey arena would be the focal point of the project, but they wanted it to be a landmark piece of the downtown area.

That building is Nationwide Arena in downtown Columbus, Ohio. With the expansion Blue Jackets set to begin play in 2000, city officials wanted a catalyst building for seventy-five acres of mixed use development in their downtown. The goal was to create a friendly building that fit well contextually within the community.

More than twenty years later, Nationwide's Arena District is considered one of the benchmark projects of its kind. It's a thriving neighborhood teeming with office and residential spaces, along with a plethora of restaurants and bars. Game nights in C-Bus are truly an experience that every NHL fan needs to experience at some point. (Tell the friendly folks at R Bar I say hi.)

Looking back on it now, Ralston says, "We kind of cracked the nut on how to allow these buildings to become part of their community, while also dispelling a lot of myths."

The goal of the Rogers Place project was not to redevelop a downtown area. Instead, officials wanted to construct an iconic building intended to make a statement and be seen from various directions. At the same time, it had to fit within an existing downtown core.

In order to find his way through the project, Ralston had to look at it through a variety of lenses. While every project has a different roadmap, he uses the same three-step approach to help him focus on the overall scope of that particular situation, and pulls them all together to come up with the final design.

What type of building will it be?

We need to do a deep dive into the science of how the building will operate. It's an event center, so we think through all of the types of events that are going to go on. Not just hockey, but everything else imaginable. And we create layers and layers of strategies for supporting those events, just physically supporting the events. What makes great ice? What makes for a great concert with an end stage? What makes for a great concert with the center stage? Then you layer on all the other types of events you can imagine and you develop a profile. Not every building is exactly alike, because not every building has a similar profile. Some buildings may have a really small seating bowl because it's focused around a basketball court, but you can still do end stage concerts. In the case of Edmonton, it was hockey first and concerts second. That helps us set the event floor.

What is the area like around the building?

It is very important to take into consideration all of the exterior stimulus. Where is it going to be located in the city? What does the city need? How does the community want to benefit from this new venue? Projects like this can go one of two paths. There's kind of a fork in the road, and we call them object buildings or background buildings. The city of Edmonton identified in their downtown plan that they wanted high design. This came out of their downtown plan in 2010, and we started design in 2011. The area around where the arena would be had an art museum and an event center and the art museum. Because of the amount of money being put into the project, they wanted an object building, an iconic building that would have an artistic presence in the city. But it also needed to fit well and work with the vehicular movement patterns and pedestrian movement patterns, and solve all the parking issues. Because if it doesn't, it becomes deadly. And there's a lot of examples of deadly buildings in North America in urban and suburban areas. In this case, the simplest way to put it is that we needed to create an iconic building that fit well within the current city grid.

Plan the seating bowl.

Now that you know the exterior stimulus, you plan for where people may be coming into the building. That also involves the event floor, so you've got to create that seating bowl that connects the public realm outside the building to the actual event floor itself. That becomes your seating bowl, and the concourse area spins off of that. There's an opportunity in each project to be very creative with all of this, so we work closely with design specialists that focus on event floors, seating bowls, and exteriors.

Ralston points to the Winter Garden as a truly unique feature of the Rogers Place project. Not only is it the primary entrance to the arena that spans over 104th Avenue in downtown Edmonton, but it's also a climate-controlled, twenty-four-thousand-square foot multiuse space that can be used for a variety of programming uses. And if you see the building from above, it was artistically designed in an oil drop formation.

NHL INVOLVEMENT

If you think these architectural firms are flying blind when it comes to designing an arena for sports programming, guess again. Both the NHL and NBA have a distinct set of design guidelines that must be incorporated into each project. While the NBA is more onerous about what they require, each league has created design standards for everything from camera positions and press level accommodations, to TV and radio broadcast positions, GM boxes, visiting GM boxes, and security outposts.

The NHL standards guide is a thoroughly detailed and evolving document that is updated annually. The league's collective bargaining agreement actually comes into play here, as there's a lot of focus on hockey operations and minimum requirements for the players.

More specifically, the CBA has specific minimum requirements that apply to how visiting teams are to be accommodated in road buildings. With the home teams already going out of their way to look after their own players in state-of-the-art locker rooms and surrounding lounges, the NHL standards guide establishes the minimum requirements for the visiting team. Which should be interesting when Arizona plays its home games in a five thousand-seat building that was designed for a college hockey program.

Designing for fluid movement within the building isn't restricted to the spectators. Keeping the "paths of travel" as separate as possible is a major concern.

"We need to figure out where the visiting team is going to arrive and how will their equipment manager move the cases through the building. Certainly you're not going to walk them through the home team area," says Ralston. "If possible, you don't want the players to cross at all. Everything involving the players is all about accommodations, movement, and safety."

As expected, the NHL guidelines focus extensively on operations, especially as it pertains to the quality of the ice, dehumidification, and overall quality of the environment. There also needs to be league-wide consistency in each building with the performance of the dashers and glass, along with specific requirements for the team benches and penalty box areas.

Another area that gets a considerable amount of attention, and rightly so, is technology. The ability to produce a world-class broadcast is vital to the league's success, making it imperative that every building can accommodate the needs of both the local and national media outlets.

Camera position requirements are significant, but there's a fair amount of flexibility in that because not every seating bowl can accommodate every fixed position that the NHL requires.

"The NHL kind of handpicked all the best camera positions— high angle, low angle, slash—for all the venues in the league years ago. But there's not one bowl that can satisfy all of those requirements," Ralston says. "It's a give and take. The league is still trying to get more low-angle cameras and lower in the bowl. But then you've got to worry about sight lines and people's hands getting in the way."

It's not just about the cameras. Because there are radio broadcasts and other forms of media at work for each event, there's also the issue of cabling. Factoring in the ideal location of junction boxes throughout the building, both inside and out, is also a significant lift.

The outside areas surrounding the building also require significant attention when planning. There needs to be dedicated spaces for all the broadcast production vehicles to park, keeping in mind the overflow they get into postseason, and that number only increases around the Finals.

"Sometimes in these urban areas you don't have a line of sight to satellites for the uplink. So you have to figure out pathways to get that link connectivity. Our work extends often well beyond the perimeter of the arena sight because you've got to think about all the people and trucks and equipment that are driving the show, the broadcast," Ralston says. "And you've got to integrate that in a way that the people that have paid for a ticket in the building aren't disturbed by all that activity. The cameras, you know, if you want to find them, you can find them. But you try to do it, that they're not blocking anybody's view or disturbing anybody's experience."

As the construction wraps up at each building, Ralston says the next step is the commissioning phase. This is when they start turning everything on to get the building in working order. The NHL staff will be on-site doing measurements and readings, and checking to see how things are going when the ice plant is fired up for the first time. They'll even run through some broadcast tests to ensure a smooth start to the season.

But just like any new home build, there are always some last-minute hiccups. Ralston found this out just as they were buttoning up Rogers Place.

"A new rule was put in place about installing a camera right over the goal line and each end. So we were just a few months from the building opening and we had to fashion a metal box with a camera in it and get it set up. But I had to do it in a way that when a show rigger for a concert came in, they wouldn't hit the camera and knock it out of position. So you know, goofy things like that, things evolve. These buildings are quite dynamic in that way."

3

SKATING

If you really think about it, the person that came up with the concept for the game of hockey was kind of nuts. Let's create a game played on ice where the participants wear boots with three-millimeter steel blades on the bottom, while using sticks to propel a piece of galvanized rubber into a net. Not exactly the most romantic of scenarios.

But to know hockey is to truly understand the magic of a steel blade caressing a clean sheet of ice. That unmistakable sound of the steel digging in to the ice, creating a new groove, and forging a path forward (or backwards) to unchartered territory.

As a kid, there was nothing better than being the first person on the ice at practice to christen that shimmering ice surface. Not much changes as you get older. If you ever get the chance to attend an NHL practice or morning skate, check out the first players that hit the ice that day. To a man, they always seem to have that same glimmer in their eye as they did as a child.

Someone who gets that look in his eye on a nightly basis is Edmonton superstar Connor McDavid. In the 2021–22 NHLPA Player Poll, McDavid was voted the one skater you'd want on your team if you need to win one game, handily defeating Sidney Crosby with 42.4 percent of the popular vote.

The numbers don't lie when it comes to McDavid's offensive dominance. The two-time MVP and three-time scoring champion has topped the 100-point plateau in five of his first seven seasons, averaging an astounding 1.4 points per game.

But it's McDavid's skating that has set him apart from his peers at a young age. McDavid, who has been clocked at straightway speeds of twenty-five miles per hour, is a lethal cocktail of power, sudden movements, the ability to change direction at a moment's notice, while not giving away anything with his eyes.

What's most remarkable is that McDavid is doing this while carrying the puck on his stick and playing a contact sport, or at least that's what the opposition is trying to do to him. McDavid consistently leaves defenders flat-footed and baffled by his remarkable power and edgework.

One of McDavid's signature moments came at home on November 5, 2021, against the New York Rangers.

As McDavid collected the puck, he slowly circled back in the neutral zone, gained speed, and proceeded to bull his way through four Rangers defenders to score the game-tying goal. The crowd noise at Rogers Place audibly increased as McDavid left each Rangers player in his wake, culminating in a roaring explosion when he slid the puck past a helpless Alexandar Georgiev.

Hockey Hall of Famer Paul Kariya was also known as a speed merchant during a fifteen-year NHL career that saw him tally 989 points in 989 games with Anaheim, Colorado, Nashville, and St. Louis. In an interview with *The Athletic* in May 2022, even he admitted there is something almost otherworldly about the man that the Oilers faithful refer to as "McJesus."

"A few people have made the analogy that he's like a video game player. It's his lateral movement, his change of direction, change of pace, and his ability to create space from guys who are trying to check him. Whether he's stopping or accelerating or changing direction, he just creates so much space with his speed, it's just incredible to watch.

"Part of it is the way he's just not fast in a straight line. He's fast side to side, stopping, starting, cutting. It just seems like once he makes a move, his ability to accelerate out of that move is beyond anyone else. If you were trying to create the perfect hockey player, that's the type of speed you want."

PHYSICS

It's safe to say that Sir Isaac Newton never played the game of hockey, yet some of his finest work can help explain the sport's intricacies.

Explaining the process of skating is a perfect example. Each time you take a stride, you are pushing on the ice. At the same time, the ice is pushing back at you. Say hello to Newton's Third Law—the law of action and reaction. When two bodies interact, they apply forces to one another that are equal in magnitude and opposite in direction.

As you begin to skate from a standing position, the goal is to accelerate as quickly as possible. To make this happen you are really pushing backwards behind you, and your blades need to be quite open for that.

"As you gain speed, you'll notice the skater is pushing more sideways. It's not exactly sideways, otherwise you'll get a lateral force on the side," explains Alain Haché. "It's slightly open, but this angle of the opening goes down as the speed picks up. You'll see speed skaters pushing almost sideways on each stride, but it's slightly open to produce a frontwards push."

Haché also says it's impossible to run as fast as you skate. When you run, you are always pushing backwards. But that would be impossible with skating. The reason we can exceed the speed of running by skating is because our legs don't have to move as fast as we are actually moving because we are pushing sideways.

For maximum acceleration at the beginning, a player will usually be very low to the ice because they need to lean forward more because the acceleration is higher.

"To maintain the equilibrium, they have to be leaning forward with a lower center of gravity. As you reach a more steady speed, then you can start being more upright," says Haché. "Your body position will depend on how fast you're accelerating. It's the same thing when you're turning, especially making a sharp turn, because you're leaning into it."

Having a much lower center of gravity also comes into play with the first few strides when skating backwards, because it's essential to get as much acceleration as possible in a short amount of time.

Skating backwards is one of the most difficult techniques to learn, and Haché says there's a very reasonable explanation why.

"I think it really just comes down to biomechanics, just like backwards running is not as efficient as going forward. The muscles and the skeleton are just not designed to efficiently do that, so for most players you'll see a considerable difference in the speed when skating backwards.

BIOMECHANICS

While McDavid has become must-see television for fans around the world, he's also caught the eye of the coaching community. Someone that has been paying close attention to McDavid for a number of years now is Dr. Mike Bracko, a power skating coach and sports psychologist with The Hockey Institute in Calgary, Alberta.

Bracko regularly uses video of NHL players to enhance his teaching, especially with younger players, and McDavid has become a popular subject during these video sessions. But it's not just the kids that are getting the education; Bracko often finds himself in awe of the things that McDavid does night in and night out.

"When you talk about McDavid, who's probably in everyone's top five list in terms of watching skate, it just blows me away how he can accelerate so quickly from a standing position."

Bracko says there's a combination of things at play here, and the first element doesn't really have a lot to do with the actual technique and biomechanics of skating. Just because a player has above-average skating ability doesn't automatically give him elite speed. It's as much about being able to generate a lot of power in their muscles.

"For McDavid, it has to do more with his raw muscle power. Generally speaking, we could say that a player with elite-level speed has a higher composition of what we call fast twitch muscle fibers. These fibers contract really fast and they are built for short, powerful bursts of energy while he skates. It's this muscle power that definitely sets McDavid apart."

The second element that Bracko focuses on while watching McDavid are the biomechanics of skating, or how the body is working in concert to complete a task.

In terms of watching McDavid, the best way to explain this is that when he is starting from a stationary position, he's externally rotating his hips to turn his toe out, so that he can push straight back on the first two or three strides.

Next up is the arm movement, which is often an overlooked factor in skating. The faster your arms move, the faster your legs move, making this a key to acceleration.

Bracko says that McDavid's muscle power and biomechanics also contribute to his ability to accelerate quickly from a gliding position.

"Just because a player can accelerate quickly from a standing position doesn't mean they can do it while gliding. But McDavid accomplishes this by using his muscle power in two components. One is that he's got the muscle power that allows him to push off and generate speed quicker. But his muscle power also allows him to get his skate back on the ice after he pushes off, which is called the recovery phase."

RECOVERY TIME

Something that a lot of younger players struggle with early on is the high-recovery phase, meaning when they push off, they'll bring the skate up really high. If you're looking at them from the front, their skate will come so high that their knee will be flexed in a way that the skate almost disappears behind their leg, giving them a high recovery.

If the skate comes up too high before getting back down in the ice, it's going to take longer for that skate to get back on the ice. Therefore it will take more time to push off again, eventually translating that player into a slower skater.

Bracko incorporates a pair of drills to teach the lower, quicker recovery. One involves the player skating down the ice and dragging their toe with each stride. The thought process behind this is to train the muscles to stay close to the ice during recovery and not bring the leg back up.

For players with a narrow stride that is typically characteristic of a slower skater, Bracko will set up a long line of five cones on the ice and the player will literally skate over top of the cones. This encourages them to have a wider stride, and it also forces them to get their skate back on the ice quicker because of the wide stride.

Another NHL player that Bracko enjoys watching is Colorado's Nathan MacKinnon, who put on a skating masterclass in the 2022 Stanley Cup playoffs. His strong and authoritative stride was on full display late in Game 5 of Colorado's second-round series against St. Louis.

MacKinnon went end to end to give Colorado a 4–3 lead with his third goal of the game, galloping like a determined thoroughbred along the back straightaway of Churchill Downs.

"MacKinnon is just so powerful and aggressive when he skates. He's got the classic biomechanics of a fast skater," says Bracko. "You can't help but notice his wide stride and quick recovery, along with a very deep knee bend. He also moves his arms side to side, just like the laws of physics explain. For every action, there's an equal and opposite reaction."

In fact, MacKinnon checks many of the boxes on Bracko's list of the top five characteristics of a fast skater:

1. Arms move side-to-side
2. Wide stride with lots of space between skates
3. Low recovery after push-off

4. Quickly getting the skate on the ice after push-off
5. The recovery skate lands in a line with shoulder-hip-knee, allowing them to get on an inside edge for push-off.

COMMON CORE

All the movements involved in a skating stride really originate from the core. You've got the shoulders and arm movement going side to side, and then the legs will move in concert with that. That's also tied into the lower body strength and the ability to strengthen the balance and the push off for everything to all come together.

In terms of skating, it's not necessarily that the core is initiating the movement. It's more about the core being able to stabilize everything, so that the player can have good leg movement, hip movement, and shoulder movement.

Deferring back to the laws of physics once more, Bracko also emphasizes how a strong core region enables the player to move his or her arms in an equal and opposite reaction with their legs.

"If they have good core strength, they'll be able to maintain their core in a position known as the neutral spine," Bracko explains. "This is the position of the spine when the cervical (neck), thoracic (middle), and lumbar (lower) regions are positioned in an ideal alignment. A neutral spine provides the most strength and allows for more natural body movements."

Specifically how it relates to the forward stride, possessing a strong core will also enable a skater to keep their trunk and torso as still as possible. It's not perfectly still, but it is relatively stable and not moving back and forth. But the core can remain relatively stationary. There is a little bit of rotation of the spine happening, but it's ever so slightly. Bracko says this is referred to lateral flexion, where there's sideways movement primarily in the neck and spine regions.

TOOLS OF THE TRADE

Many years ago it was noteworthy if a player didn't wear socks in his skates, or left the top few eyelets undone to give himself more flexibility in the ankle area. Not to mention, the skates were heavier and the blades were mounted on steel tubes.

These days the players are wearing custom-fitted skates built from space-age materials that are designed specifically for their stride, and the skates weigh no more than a loaf of bread. Although they do cost significantly more than a loaf of bread, with a high-end pair of skates now costing big dough, typically in the $1,000 range.

And similar to how the stick market has been trending over the years, skate manufacturers continue to put an emphasis on making their products lighter, while catering to the specific needs of the user.

"From our standpoint, it always starts with consumer research and the biomechanics of the skating stride. It's important to understand how the game is being taught for the next generation of skaters and for today's elite-level players," says John Davidson, senior brand manager of skates for Bauer Hockey. "What we've been able to decipher is that a skater can typically be separated into two key categories. Some players are considered to be a powerful skater, using a more technical method that leverages range of motion to be able to get the most out of their legs on each and every stride. And then you have a player that focuses more on quickness and agility. Think of that as being a player that is a little more shifty going left and right, or east to west, rather than the powerful north to south style."

By using this information, Bauer is able to design each model to fit a particular style of skater, catering to the desired output of the user.

Looking at Bauer's Vapor model, there's a lot of flexibility in the boot, with more of it occurring in the lower back portion. That makes it a little bit more reactive, allowing players to move east and west a little bit easier.

While the top portion of the boot is more stiff and supportive, it's also softer or more flexible in the bottom back portion of the boot to give it that certain flex point in the skate to make it more reactive. These type of players tend to look for a skate with more support as they're shifting from left to right. So again, it's that combination of the two that really make it the ultimate skate for that kind of player.

The Vapor is also manufactured with materials that are a lot stiffer in the eyelet area, giving it that optimal stiffness in that particular location. It's this stiffness that provides a little bit more support throughout the skating stride.

That being said, some flex notches have been added to make sure the ankle still has the ability to flex. The materials used to manufacture the Vapor provides a little bit more stability up in the top portion of the foot.

Bauer's Supreme model emphasizes more of a power component. The bottom of the boot is much more integrated and stiffer than a Vapor, but the top portion is much more flexible.

Some flex notches have been integrated into the boot, allowing your ankle to act as the hinge and flex the top of the boot, offering as much range of motion as the skater requires. With the bottom of the boot being stiffer, it's helping to transfer energy throughout the entire skating stride.

Even the foam tongue of the skate can add another layer of functionality to the skate, with twenty-five different variations made available to players at the NHL level. A thicker tongue can provide more protection and support, while some are thinner and lighter.

Davidson says there's no real science behind a choice of tongue, with it really coming down to personal preference on how they want it customized.

"For some guys it really comes down to them being a creature of habit and what makes the skate most comfortable for them. Some players like a really soft tongue and some players like a really stiff one, depending on how they want it to flex during their stride. It's definitely the one part of the skate that is the most interchangeable, but it's hard to actually figure out why one player likes it different from another."

BLADE RUNNERS

To get anywhere on a pair of skates, you'll need one vital component: the blade. The three-millimeter wide steel runners are affixed to a plastic holder that is mounted to the bottom of the boot.

A skate blade has to be smooth in order to reduce the friction with the ice, so the process of sharpening is done to minimize any surface roughness. Friction between steel and ice is very small in the first place, so it's actually a good thing that blades are made of steel.

Because of the back and forth direction of the skating stride, you want as much glide as possible, so this is where the narrow blade comes in handy.

As the blade applies pressure on the ice, it will in some cases melt some water underneath it and therefore make it even more slippery. That water will freeze again after the blade passes over it.

The blade has a hollow groove underneath that is basically shaped like an inverse U. The purpose of this is to make each side to be as sharp as possible because you want very high resistance laterally.

"Because if you are going to push and accelerate, you will need to tilt your skate and apply pressure or force sideways in order to propel yourself forward, so you want a good grip," says Haché. "It's when you lose some of that sharp edge is when you'll start slipping. That very specific design is good for very low friction front and back, but very high friction sideways. That's what you want for maximum traction."

The width of the skate blade itself is not much of a problem, because if you put the two skates side to side, it's the width between the skates that matters in terms of keeping your equilibrium. If you're standing on your skates in a comfortable position, you have the two anchor points that provide the balance.

Keeping your balance on skates may look like a difficult task on the narrow blades, regardless of your skill level. But as Haché explains, it's not as daunting as it looks.

"When a tree starts falling, it falls very slowly. It's the inertia of rotation that prevents it from falling quickly. It's that same inertia of rotation that allows the person to be upright. With the brain constantly making adjustments, it can detect even the slightest changes of orientation. Even without thinking, the muscle will make sure you don't just lean and fall and tip over. Ice skating is the same premise."

STAYING SHARP

Having sharp skates is the key to getting the most out of your experience. Sharpening skates creates the edges needed to grip the ice, while also removing any nicks or slight imperfections to the blade that could add friction between the ice and steel. Let's face it—without the proper edges, you might as well be wearing socks on a newly waxed floor.

In order to sharpen skates, the blade is passed over a grinding wheel at a slow, consistent speed, starting with the toe and moving to the heel. There's no industry standard, but it can take anywhere from three to five passes of the blade to complete the sharpening. Some NHL equipment staffers will go as high as eight.

Before the sharpening begins, the radius is preset to create the particular hollow that the skater wants on the blade. The easiest way to explain the hollow is that it's the space between the two edges of a skate blade. Each blade has an inside edge and an outside edge (thanks Captain Obvious), with the space in between making up the hollow.

Using a smaller radius, also known as a deeper hollow, enables more glide to the stride, but it can also compromise the grip or bite the blade needs to make sudden stops. In terms of measurements, these would be in the range of five-eighths to one inch.

In turn, a larger radius offers a blunter edge with a smaller hollow (one half inch, three eighths of an inch), providing maximum grip during turns but offering less glide for the speed component.

A typical sharpening, especially for youth hockey players, is the standard one half inch recommended by most hockey pro shops.

As for the frequency of sharpenings, that really comes down to personal preference. Some players judge it by the frequency of their ice time, while others just prefer to maintain a consistent feel to their blades by getting it done more often.

SPACE AGE STEEL

Bauer offers three different types of steel runners for their skates, starting with the Pulse. This steel is the baseline version that is very similar to how steel has been constructed for years. It's not lightweight by any means, but it's very durable.

It has a high polish finish on the outside, and that finish is what gives you a better kind of glide during the skating stride. It actually reduces the amount of friction that interacts with the ice, allowing the skater to maintain their glide for a longer period of time.

When you go from the Pulse to the Pulse TI, it has a physical coating on the outside rather than a polished finish. This physical coating is a titanium material that bonds to the core steel material. The Pulse and Pulse TI are actually the exact same steel, but the difference is the coating on the outside of the steel provides a harder outside edge.

So when you go in to push off, what you'll notice with the TI is that because of those harder edges, you can really kind of dig in and take off a little bit easier with it.

The hardness of those edges also makes the steel retain its sharpening for a longer period of time, and this is known as edge retention. The duration of that retention varies from anywhere from 10 to 20 percent, and it really depends on how hard someone is on their blades and kind of the skating motions they have.

Bauer's top-end runner is the Carbonlite, a completely rethought of and reengineered type of steel that is 25 percent lighter than a traditional blade.

What sets the Carbonlite apart is a bridge material on the top of the steel that is made from carbon fiber—the same material used to manufacture sticks. The carbon fiber adds increased torsional flex, similar to how a stick can bend when taking a shot. This adds to the power and acceleration in every stride.

Using carbon fiber can actually change the flex profile of the particular object that you're creating. While the blade still maintains the same lateral stiffness as a traditional steel, it is basically the carbon fiber grabbing the steel and trying to flex it and bend it side to side.

It still has the same lateral stiffness to contribute to the long stride output, but the torsional stiffness is a little bit more flexible. While not visible to the naked eye, that torque from the carbon fiber will give you a little bit of a kick as you start your push off, and allow you to move left to right a little bit quicker in the agility strides. Similar to how a stick flex provides more whip and power to a shooter, the Carbonlite blade actually does some of the work for you.

FOOT FOR THOUGHT

The current weight of Bauer's Vapor Hyperlite skate is about 1.5 pounds, which is 25 percent lighter than the Vapor model from just twenty years ago.

When it comes to their skates, the average NHL player will go through about six pairs each season. But a player referred to as a "heavy user" can use as many as twenty-five pairs. Then there are players like Johnny Gaudreau and Taylor Hall who may only break in about one or two pairs each season.

4

SHOOTING

Scoring is on the rise in the NHL. As the game evolves, so do the shooters. The elite players are always looking for a way to bulge the twine. It takes more than just a new stick to get the job done. Finding the back of the net means you have to outthink your opponent, using every tool in your arsenal to light the lamp.

That's where Tim Turk comes in.

Turk has been a shooting and skills consultant for several NHL teams, including Montreal, Carolina, Calgary, and Tampa Bay. It's his job to help shooters unlock their full potential and get to that next level. Turk also knows his tips and tricks can do more than just make a scoreboard work overtime. Becoming an elite goal scorer usually means a bigger payday, making the difference between the league minimum and a superstar salary.

It's the accuracy element of shooting that is the most dynamic. For example, when a player fires the puck short side over the goalie's shoulder as he's leaning on the post, there's basically a four-by-four inch gap that the puck can go through. Even while dealing with speed and contact, there's no denying the skill involved in making that shot.

"You'll hear the announcer say, 'That was the only place he could put it.' And he's right. The shooter knew exactly where that was going," Turk explains. "Pinpoint accuracy at the NHL level is a one-foot box. If you can shoot the puck in five-on-five hockey in a one-foot box with only a second or two to prepare, that's pinpoint accuracy and you're making five million dollars a year."

EVOLUTION OF THE STICK

For every hockey player, finding the right stick is one of the most important parts of the game. If you want to start making those millions of dollars in the pros, you'll need to find that sweet spot of how the stick feels in your hands and how it responds when you handle the puck.

The evolution of the hockey stick is actually pretty remarkable to look back on. The heavy, two-piece stick made its debut in the 1920s when Hespeler patented the design where a blade was inserted into the bottom of the shaft.

Canadian manufacturer CCM (which stands for Canada Cycle and Motor) had already been making sticks from ash and elm trees, but they developed a laminated version in 1935. Employee Ernie Everden patented a three-piece stick where the blade and shaft were separate pieces of wood held together like a puzzle using waterproof glue and a wooden wedge. Not only did this expedite the manufacturing process, it also eliminated waste as any smaller pieces could be used in making the multiple parts, rather than being discarded.

A 1935 CCM ad in a sporting goods catalogue stated: "Boiling, steaming and bending are eliminated, thus the woods retain all of the natural strength qualities which they possessed in the tree."

In case you're wondering, a typical stick in this era weighed about twenty-six ounces, or 737 grams. As you'll find out later on, this is twice the weight of Bauer's top of the line Hyperlite carbon fiber model.

The innovations didn't stop there, as a company called Northland started wrapping the blade in fiberglass to increase its strength in the 1950s.

As the years went on, stick manufacturers began using fiberglass to reinforce that shaft of the stick. Not only did this made the stick lighter, it also lowered manufacturing costs.

Stick options started to increase in the 1970s as more companies started producing them. Newcomers Sher-Wood and Canadien began to take over the market, making sticks from aspen wood and reinforcing them with fiberglass to make sticks even lighter

Sticks also became a popular marketing tool in the 1980s, with manufacturers like Koho and Titan joining the fray and aligning themselves with some of the game's superstars to create almost iconic brand awareness.

Wayne Gretzky was actually at the forefront of two of the most recognizable hockey sticks in hockey history. The Great One's white Titan stick with the red lettering became a must-have item for kids of all ages looking to emulate their hero.

When Easton launched its aluminum shafted stick in the late '80s, they turned to Gretzky for instant brand recognition, as the shiny silver shaft glistened under the glare of arena lights.

While slightly heavier and stiffer than the wood and fiberglass sticks being used at the time, the product offered incredible durability and users had the ability to simply swap out the fiberglass blade that popped into the base of the shaft.

The true game-changing moment for hockey sticks was the launch of the Easton Synergy one-piece composite stick in 2000. These lighter and more responsive sticks made from carbon fiber have added another dimension to the game.

Just like a golfer getting more length off the tee with a fancy new driver, the materials used to manufacture a one-piece composite stick continue to benefit shooters and befuddle goaltenders.

STICK TO IT

Weight is definitely a major driver of performance in a composite stick, and that's one of the driving forces behind Bauer's Hyperlite, one of their high-end models that is used by players throughout the NHL. The lighter the stick, the faster that the stick will recoil. So essentially, when you're loading the stick, the faster that it will go from being fully loaded back to its original point to release the puck off the blade.

"At its core, the driver of that weight is really about carbon fiber," says Tyson Teplitsky, senior brand manager for Bauer Hockey. "It's really the evolution of what we've been able to utilize from a carbon fiber standpoint that that has helped us dramatically reduce the weight. And with the way carbon fiber is structured, it also helps with the overall performance of the stick."

The Hyperlite is 100 percent carbon fiber construction all the way through the entire stick. But it's not just the fact that it's all carbon fiber, it's the thickness of the carbon fiber layers and how those layers are stacked within the internal structure of the stick.

Utilizing really high-end, high-impact carbon fiber on the external part of the construction of the sticks on the layer that you actually see helps not only with reducing the weight, but also helps with the impact and the durability of the structure.

"For us, we can always drive the weight down but it always has to make sense. We are constantly walking a tightrope when it comes to weight. We can make sticks incredibly light, but if they blow up on every shot, that doesn't make much sense from a business standpoint," says Teplitsky. "So it is finding that balance of creating a structure where we are chasing a light weight, which for the most part is the name of the game in today's hockey world for all the hockey manufacturers, while not sacrificing and making sure that the sticks are going to last a long enough time where consumers aren't going to get upset. It's a value proposition for us."

When you watch a player exerting so much pressure and force on the stick, it's almost incredible that it doesn't blow up on every shot, especially with a stick like the Hyperlite that only weighs about 350 grams (about .75 pounds). But the true key to the stick's durability is the Duraflex resin used in the shaft.

The resin combines with the stacked layers of carbon fiber layers to hold the structure together while adding durability to the product. Teplitsky says that the resin used in the Hyperlite is often described as the stick's windshield.

"If you throw a rock at a windshield, it will crack, but in most cases the rock is not going to come right through. And ideally, once that crack starts, it's not just going to expand throughout your entire windshield. That's kind of like the way that the resin is built within that structure of the stick. If you get slashed, you might get a little crack in the shaft based off of that. But the resin is going to try to help mitigate the spreading of that crack to make the stick lasts as long as possible."

Utilizing the right combination of resin and carbon fiber is not only essential for the weight of the stick, but it also comes into play with the load and release of shot. Being able to get the ideal flex and whip from the stick is what a goal scorer is looking for.

The lighter weight is what everyone wants, but the shooter needs to know how much force they can exert on the shaft during the load process to help create the whip in the release without snapping it in half.

As the player is in the shooting motion, they will lean their lower hand into it, and essentially let the stick do some of the work for them with the whip during the release. Having confidence in both the stick and their own ability is what ultimately takes over, making the resin a key factor in the construction of sticks.

"That's really kind of a big shift that you've seen in hockey over the past little while. The way that technology is and has enhanced with sticks, it means that the stick does a lot of the work now for the player. If the stick works like they expect it to, then they don't have to put as much energy into that stick to be able to get as much power into their shots."

FLEX TIME

You may not have thought of it this way, but Turk likes to say that a stick is just an extension of your body. And to have success in hockey, players really need to find that sweet spot with both the length and flex of the stick they decide to go to battle with.

With so many styles and options available to them, finding that success is going to take time to figure out. A lot of it will depend on the position you play, and some it will also be contingent on your physical stature and skill level.

"Once you're confident with a stick, you now have the confidence with it for any kind of shot in any situation. For me, it took a lot of trial by error to finally figure out what was perfect," explains Jeff Serowik, who had a 10-year pro career that featured NHL stops on defense with Toronto, Boston, and Pittsburgh. "But once you get it down, it does make a huge difference. It does make you feel a lot more comfortable on the ice when you're shooting."

The flex of a stick, basically how much it will bend, is something that a lot players struggle with early on. It may look cool to be able to bend the stick and add a few miles per hour to your shot, but it can sometimes lead to control issues on your shots, along with issues in your bank account because you keep breaking them.

In simplest terms, the higher a flex, the stiffer the stick is. So naturally, a lower flex number will be a whippier stick. The flex number represents how many pounds of force are required to bend the stick.

One rule of thumb in figuring out your ideal flex number is to take your body weight in pounds, and divide that by two. Using this logic, a person that weighs 180 pounds would be looking to use a 90 flex. Of course it's all about personal preference, but at least now you've got a starting point to work with.

In the eyes of Turk, his simple rule of thumb is "if you can't flex your stick more than two full inches, it's too stiff. The stick needs to be flexed so the 'kick' return can project the puck."

When it comes to NHL players, their flex preferences are all over the map, and don't necessarily correspond to their playing weight. Tampa Bay's Nikita Kucherov is listed as 5-foot-11 and 183 pounds. However, he typically plays with a 62 flex because he wants to be able to get a shot off quickly in tight situations without changing his hand positioning.

Like Kucherov, Alex Ovechkin unloads his rockets with a flex that is nowhere near what the target number would be. Despite checking in at 6-foot-3 and 235 pounds, "The Great Eight" has been known to use a flex in the eighty range, making it look like he's playing with a pool noodle at times. But when you're considered one of the greatest goal scorers of all time, I guess we'll have to take Ovie's word for it that it's a comfortable stick.

On the flipside of this is the hulking 6-foot-9 defenseman Zdeno Chara. Adding to his height is a weight that tips the scales at around 250 pounds, easily making him one of the most powerful players in the game. Throughout his storied career, Chara has been known to use sticks with a flex ranging from 110 to 150, a model that Serowik describes as "basically playing with an oak tree in your hands."

Serowik started his career using a 75 flex, which wasn't exactly ideal for his 180-pound frame. Not only did he find it difficult to catch passes with, he was breaking a lot of sticks. Every so often he'd unleash a bomb with it, but said the negatives definitely outweighed the positives.

"It took some time but I finally found my most comfortable stick. I'd get an 85 and cut it down to the perfect length where it turns into a 90. [Cutting a stick by an inch or two can increase a flex by about 10.]

"That length is huge too. Defensemen usually have their stick cut at their nose for some added length. Forwards normally have it up to their chin or lips to help with puck control. Finding that perfect combination of flex and length is kind of the biggest challenge as far as sticks wise, because it truly does make a difference."

USE THE FORCE

Don't be fooled by the explanation of the new sticks doing a lot of the work for a player. It still takes a lot of work and skill to become an elite goal scorer in the NHL. Alain Haché of the University of Moncton (New Brunswick) has done extensive studies on how physics are involved with the game of hockey.

When it comes to shooting the puck, Haché explains that the work always starts with the shooter.

"The stick itself doesn't provide any energy. The work is really being done by the athlete, and you want to do it as efficiently as possible. A lot of it has to do with positioning and how you're going to flex the stick before making contact with the puck. If you do a direct stick on puck collision, then you will get some transfer. But it won't be anywhere near as much as if you store more energy inside the stick by flexing it.

"It also depends on the type of shot you are taking. If it's a wrist shot, you can apply the force to bend the stick much easier than if you do a slap shot. Sticks now are more efficient than in the old days when they were made with materials that were not quite optimum for that. If you used an old-style wooden stick, you would lose energy in the transfer, as opposed to what players are using now."

Being on the move is key to increasing the speed of a shot. Being able to make a goalie move out of position is paramount to creating a scoring chance. And with the puck now in motion, it will add some extra velocity to the shot.

Haché explains how this works: "If you are skating with the puck and shooting, then the velocity the puck already has will be added on to the speed you are giving it with the shot itself. That's why you'll have a faster shot as you move towards the net. Whereas if you have a defenseman that is almost standing still at the blue line, his shot will be less because he's shooting a puck that is starting from a resting position.

"However, if the puck is passed to that defenseman and he takes a one-timer, it's been known that you'll get a faster shot because of what's known as the rebound effect. Once he takes that shot, he'll use the power he applies to the shot plus the rebound effect from the moving pass. It's similar to a pitcher throwing to a batter in baseball. If you are hitting a stationary ball, you would get less distance than if the ball had been thrown to you. When you hit a home run, it's really the combined effort of the pitcher and the batter."

OFFENSIVE EXPLOSION

With all the goals that were scored in 2021–22, goaltenders must've been constantly treating sunburn on their necks from all the red lights going off behind them. In the first full 82- game schedule in three years, the NHL posted its highest scoring season since 1995–96 with a total of 8,150 goals scored, an average of 6.3 per game.

As a comparison, there were 7,664 goals scored in 2018–19, which happened to be the most since coming out of the lockout in 2005–06, when an emphasis was put on creating more offense.

The 340 goals scored by Florida in 2021–22 were far and away the most in the NHL. Toronto (315), Colorado (312), St. Louis (311), and Minnesota (310) were the only other teams to break the 300-goal barrier.

And before you go thinking that the addition of a thirty-second franchise in Seattle contributed to the onslaught, just know that the expansion Kraken only scored 216 goals, the fourth fewest in the league behind Arizona (207), Philadelphia (211), and San Jose (214).

Leading the charge was Toronto's Auston Matthews, who scored a league-leading 60 goals on 348 shots. Matthews became the first United States-born player to reach the 60-goal plateau, and was the league's first 60-goal scorer since Steven Stamkos of Tampa Bay bagged 60 in 2011–12.

The 60-goal milestone has been reached forty times in league history, but only twenty-one players have accomplished it. Some guy named Wayne Gretzky scored 60 goals or more in five of six seasons from 1981 to 1987, including a mind-boggling 92 in 1981–82. Clearly, an NHL record that will never be broken.

Mike Bossy, the poster child for goal-scoring consistency throughout his career, also scored 60 or more goals five times. (Bossy scored at least 50 goals in nine of his ten seasons with the New York Islanders. A back injury forced his retirement in 1987.)

Mario Lemieux and Phil Esposito each had four seasons of 60 goals or more. These four Hall of Famers have combined for 45 percent of all 60-goal seasons in league history, and just the pairing of Gretzky and Bossy alone account for 25 percent.

What's even more remarkable about Gretzky's 92-goal-season was that he scored them on just 370 shots, for a shooting percentage of 24.86 percent.

Of the four players that scored 50 or more goals in 2021–22— Matthews, Leon Draisaitil (55), Chris Kreider (52), and Alex Ovechkin (50)—only Kreider had a shooting percentage higher than 20 at 20.2.

The 2021–22 season also had 137 20-goal scorers, the most in one season since there were 135 in 1980–81. There were also fifty-one players that recorded a 30-goal season, and seventeen finished with 40 or more.

SHOT SELECTION

There was an old Nike baseball commercial in the '90s featuring Greg Maddux and Tom Glavine proclaiming that chicks dig the long ball. The same could've been said about hockey's love affair with the booming slap shot. Stronger and harder were all the rage as hulking defensemen such as Al MacInnis, Zdeno Chara, and Shea Weber made a living out of unloading 100 mile per hour bombs from the point, much to the chagrin of terrified goaltenders and shot blockers.

Not anymore. These days, it's the wrist shot that's getting all the love in the NHL.

Of the 8,150 goals scored in 2021–22, an astonishing 4,247 (52.1 percent) of them came via the wrist shot, easily the most of all the goals documented by the NHL. The wrist shot, affectionately referred to as "the silencer" by Turk, also accounted for 47,861 (57.7 percent) of the 82,984 total shots taken leaguewide. These numbers were all up across the board when comparing them to 2018–19, the league's last full 82-game season.

In 2018–19, 3,921 goals were scored using the wrist shot, representing 51.7 percent of the league total of 7,577 goals scored. The 44,083 wrist shot attempts were also the most in the league, and made up 55.1 percent of the 79,941 total shots.

The snap shot came in second in total goals and shots both years, and also proved to be the most accurate of the two shot styles.

In 2021–22, 1,278 goals came via the snap shot on 11,129 attempts, for a shooting percentage of 11.5 percent. This was nearly 3 percent higher than the wrist shot. The snap shot also accounted for 15.7 percent of the total goals scored.

As a comparison, there were 1,146 goals scored on 11,254 attempts using the snap shot in 2018–19. These numbers calculate to a 10.2 shooting percentage and were 15.1 percent of all goals scored league-wide.

If you're wondering about our old friend the slap shot, it saw a bit of a resurgence in 2021–22. A total of 772 goals came off the clapper, twenty-eight more than in 2018–19.

However, slap shot usage was definitely down year over year. A total of 10,693 slap shot attempts were made in 2021–22, a decrease of 919 from the 11,612 attempts in 2018–19. In both years, the slap shot goal totals were just under 10 percent of the league's total goals.

Matthew Tkachuk and Matt Duchene led all NHLers with 31 wrist shot goals in 2021–22, followed by Johnny Gaudreau (30) and Tage Thompson (29). In the case of Gaudreau, his thirty wrist shot tallies represented 75 percent of his career-high 40 goals.

It should come as no surprise that the wrist shot was the weapon of choice for Matthews as he took home the Rocket Richard Trophy for a second straight season as the league's leading goal scorer, following his 41-goal campaign in the COVID-abbreviated 2020–21 season.

Of his 60 goals, 28 of them were scored using the wrist shot. Despite his reliance on the wrister, Matthews mixed in a little bit of everything in his record-setting season. His totals also featured nine goals using his backhand, eight with a snap shot, seven via a tip in front, six slapshots, and two on the wraparound.

The aforementioned Serowik is someone who truly marvels at Matthews' prowess with the puck. Having played on a Penguins team that featured future Hall of Famer Jaromir Jagr at the peak of his highlight reel career, Serowik, who now runs Pro Ambitions Hockey in Massachusetts, knows an elite talent when he sees it.

"Matthews has probably the best wrist shot in the league. If you just watch the follow through on his shot, I mean, he's just so strong. He's quick, he's deceptive, and he's able to change the angle on his shots so you never know what's coming. He can do it all AND he's 6-foot-3. He's an absolute freak."

WHAT MAKES THEM ELITE?

Just like trying to pick lottery numbers, there's no tried and true method to creating an elite goal scorer. The mental and physical makeup of a goal scorer is what keeps them at the top of their game.

Today's shooters are all about speed and deception, using their footwork as another way to keep a goalie guessing. It's no longer about trying to just fire it through the goalie, they are trying to put the pack past him using any means possible.

This doesn't mean you won't find Stamkos and Ovechkin setting up shop in the right faceoff dot and terrorizing goalies with their one-timers anymore. They've been forced to become more creative in their shot attempts. They'll still get their patented shots off, but now they've added an element of pre-shot motion to keep the defenders off guard.

Serowik has seen this trend growing in the NHL, and now it's already trickled down to the teenage and college players that he works with at his clinics.

"The days of teaching a player to take a wrist shot in a stationary position just by simply transferring their bodyweight, it's long gone. Now it's about changing lanes to take shots and opening up your hips to get people off balance and making the goalie move. There's so much more to taking a shot than ever before."

CONFIDENCE IS KEY

There are so many ways to try and figure out what makes an elite shooter tick. From the accuracy and power, to the ability to successfully make repeatable shots in the blink of an eye, night in and night out. No matter how hard you try, sometimes they just look unstoppable.

For the most part, Turk says it's all about a player having confidence. Not just in their ability, but in their overall physical makeup, the foundational confidence of how the parts of the body work in sync to perform the activity. The confidence of knowing what you want to do in your mind, and being able to execute that thought process in high-speed motion.

When it comes to the elite shooters, a lot of what they do is simply just natural ability. They don't know what they're doing well, because that's just how they are. That's the challenge Turk faces when working with certain players. He makes sure not to compromise anything they are doing, while offering up even the smallest of suggestions and opinions.

"The simplest way to explain it is that I call it foundational. It's all based on their biomechanics, what their body is doing when they do it. So if they need to modify it, maybe someone like me will come in and suggest they change their body angle by half a degree when shooting. It may seem minor, but you don't want to ruin what they've built up.

"When it comes to the NHL level, millimeters can be like a million miles when you're making these modifications and fine-tuning motion patterns."

TAKING IT IN STRIDE

The mind games between goaltenders and shooters are never ending. Shooters are always looking for new ways to score goals, and goaltenders will do whatever it takes to stop them. Whether it's a positional style or an equipment adjustment, a goaltender is always looking to stay one step ahead. But leave it to the shooter to literally get an extra step on their archnemesis.

So many of the goals scored in recent years have come out of what Turk calls the "stride formation." Combine this movement with a quick wrister or snap shot, and the shooter suddenly gets the advantage.

The premise of the stride formation is simple. If you're a lefty, your left leg goes back when you release the puck. For a righty, it's the right leg that drops back. It's like you're taking a skating stride as you're shooting. The foundation of shooting the puck is getting that leg back. By staying in motion, the goalie isn't able to square up the shooter to fill the net.

To no surprise, Turk points to Matthews as a player that executes the stride formation brilliantly and consistently.

"It's all about the lower body configuration mixed with the shot type release. But what Matthews will do is get into that formation when he's got a high rate of speed and momentum built up. Then he'll drop his leg back and pause while he's in that formation, and then he'll pull the puck laterally inward and unleash a combination of a wrist and snap shot, instead of one or the other. Some players are doing something similar, but not dropping the leg back."

Maintaining proper body alignment will add accuracy, deception, and reaction time. Even if a shooter is unable to get their leg back, whatever that posture position or power position that the stride formation has put them in, they need to mimic that and hold the posture level.

Turk explains how it's imperative not to stand up during a shot attempt, and don't bend over or lean to the side.

"Good shooters look like they explode out of their chest. That means the hips have to go back for their shoulders and chest to go forward. The stride formation sets the foundation for that. From there they can create the deception, as long as their hip and shoulder position doesn't get compromised. But that's easier said than done with all the contact that takes place during a game.

"It's easy for spine angles and the loading position to change in an instant. The preparation of the puck—what the body does before, during, and after a shot—is sometimes more important than the location of the puck itself. It's so important to be stable and reactive once the release is taken."

SIGNATURE MOVES

Keeping the goalies guessing is something that shooters have become quite adept at over the years. Players are always looking for an edge, and they've developed numerous lower body formations to go along with the multiple shot types. This includes the scissor move that's become popular where the shooter splits their legs and feet when shooting.

The idea is to try to have a signature move that a player is most effective with, but also using some variations on a theme that will make them as unpredictable as possible.

The goalie might get used to seeing a shooter's left leg drop back on a snap shot, but then they'll mess up the goalie's timing mechanism by unleashing a wrist shot instead. Just that simple fraction of a second can mean all the difference between an easy save or top-shelf snipe.

"It's important for a shooter to develop variety in their shot selection. For any good goal scorer, it's all about using your body to help change the angle of the shot, ultimately making you as unpredictable as possible to the goalie," says Turk, who counts the 2021–22 Canadian Hockey League Player of the Year, Logan Stankoven, among his many pupils. Stankoven, a second-round pick of Dallas in 2021, tallied 45 goals and 104 points for Kamloops of the Western Hockey League.

TIME AND SPACE

One of the challenges facing a shooter is being able to get the shot attempt off cleanly, while trying to avoid the defender's best attempts to thwart the opportunity at all costs. The term *creating space* is thrown around by broadcasters and analysts, but it just means the shooter has to find a way to get into an open lane as they work within the strict confines of the two hundred by eighty-five foot ice surface and the five defenders that want nothing more than to prevent the shot from happening at all.

This is a teachable skill, but one that Turk says is very challenging.

"The way you're evading the defender is not with speed or space, it's with the proper timing in a protective kind of mode. It's really about situational awareness based on what your body is doing. The less space that you take—the top hand pulls, and the bottom hand pushes—when taking a shot, the more deceptive it is. But you still have to generate the same amount of power with the pushing and pulling motion pattern."

For example, if a right-handed shot is coming down the wing against a left-handed defenseman, their sticks are lined up directly opposite each other. The shooter then has to put their body in a position that allows them to create more time for themselves, but it hasn't necessarily made more space.

A savvy forward will use an open-hip skating move that helps create more deception because it freezes or delays the defender, who is now unsure of what the attacker is about to do. He hasn't necessarily made more space or created distance, just done something where it created more time in that same space because of the blockage or shielding.

Being an elite goal scorer is about more than having a great shot. The star players nowadays can do a little bit of everything. This cat and mouse game between goalies and shooters has been going on for years, and it just keeps getting more intense.

5

GOALTENDING

There's been a lot of consternation over the years about a goal-tender's value and impact on team performance. For a position that is literally the last line of defense, it feels like there has been an overall devaluation of a goaltender's worth to a hockey team.

St. Louis won a Stanley Cup in 2019 backstopped by Jordan Binnington, a red-hot rookie who hasn't come close to matching that playoff performance in the ensuing years. Florida is paying Sergei Bobrovsky 10 million dollars a year until 2026, and he put up a pedestrian .913 save percentage in 2021–22 that ranked him just nineteenth overall.

Colorado only added fuel to the fire in 2022 by taking home a Cup with Darcy Kuemper between the pipes.

A sixth-round draft pick by Minnesota in 2009, Colorado was Kuemper's fourth team in ten seasons. While his .921 save percentage in the regular season was fifth in the league, Kuemper's 2.54 goals against average in 2021–22 wasn't even ranked in the top ten. (Kuemper added a fifth team to his résumé when he signed with Washington as a free agent in July 2022)

Ironically, some of Kuemper's numbers weren't dissimilar to Igor Shesterkin of the New York Rangers, who took home the Vezina Trophy as the league's best goaltender and finished third in voting for the Hart Trophy as MVP.

Their overall win-loss records were almost identical, with Shesterkin posting 36–13–4 totals in 53 games, and Kuemper was 37–12–4 in 57 games.

But this is where the similarities end.

Shesterkin faced 1,622 shots in those 53 games and made 1,516 saves for a league-best .935 save percentage. Shesterkin was also tops in the league with a 2.07 goals against average, well ahead of Frederik Andersen (2.17) and Jacob Markstrom (2.22).

There was already a buzz around Shesterkin's remarkable regular season when the playoffs started, but he stole the spotlight in New York's Game 1 loss to Pittsburgh when he made 79 saves in a three-OT heartbreaker.

The 26-year-old Russian ended up starting all 20 of New York's playoff games, and led the league with a .929 save percentage on 720 shots.

With so much money being paid to the game's offensive stars, it seems like some teams are willing to roll the dice on goaltending and simply try to outscore the opposition. Colorado is the case study in this, scoring 58 more goals than the Rangers in 2021–22, and running roughshod over their opponents on many nights.

Colorado had 38 wins in 2021–22 when outscoring the opposition by two or more goals. That was third in the league behind only Calgary (40) and St. Louis (39). Meanwhile, Shesterkin's Rangers won 22 games when the margin of victory was just a single goal.

While Kuemper wasn't even in the conversation for the Vezina, there's no telling where the Rangers would've been without Shesterkin in goal.

THE PERFECT MIX

Saying that goaltenders are unique individuals is being polite. It takes a special kind of person to take the abuse that a goalie does, both physically and mentally.

There is no magic formula to creating the ideal goaltender. The mental makeup is just as important as the various physical attributes that someone brings to the position. But in order to become elite, a goaltender needs to find a way to maximize their full potential in all areas.

Ian Clark knows a little bit about pulling the full potential from a goaltender. Called the "goalie guru" by many in the industry,

Clark is the director of goaltending and head goaltending coach for Vancouver. Some of his star pupils are a who's who of the NHL's goaltending fraternity, highlighted by Hall of Famer Roberto Luongo, two-time Vezina Trophy winner Sergei Bobrovsky, Jacob Markstrom, and Thatcher Demko.

Canucks prospect Mike DiPietro had high praise for Clark's coaching techniques.

"He has the ability to recognize a goalie and knows goalies don't play the exact same way. Clarkie has allowed me to still be Michael DiPietro, the goaltender who battles and competes, but also in more controlled ways, you know, having better footwork," DiPietro told Vancouver's *Province* in May 2021.

"Honestly, I cannot say enough great things about Ian Clark. He has helped my game in a tremendous way, and I know everybody that's worked with him will say the exact same thing."

In his appearance on the InGoal Radio podcast, Clark outlined his seven key components to what makes an elite goaltender:

Athleticism: The goaltender's natural ability to athletically play the position. Part of that is flexibility and elasticity. It's the ability to use athleticism to support your game. If you don't have it, you're going to struggle to hit the elite stratosphere.

Competitiveness: If you're not your team's fiercest competitor, you're going to struggle in putting that full recipe together as an elite goaltender. This includes both games and practices.

Instinctive Ability: Clark defines this as the ability to break from structure, a combination of a player's compete level and their overall creativity. The ability to find a creative solution, under pressure, in the moment. Some of the best saves made by a goalie are unique, one-off saves that may not be able to repeat because you may only make it once in your life.

Reactivity: If you can only support your inside from a coverage perspective. The ability to react and protect your outside equally as well as your inside, is an essential piece of the elite puzzle.

Technical: This could also be referred to as structural or mechanical.

Visual Talent: The ability to consistently track or follow the puck.

Technique: If the technique is repeated over and over, the goalie will undoubtedly get better at that technique.

Every goaltender is built differently, but Clark says it's how they use each of these attributes that makes them stand out from their peers.

"Marc-Andre Fleury may be a guy that has a full cup of technique, but Marty Brodeur only had two tablespoons of technique. But if you want to talk about a competitor, and you want to talk about instincts, goaltending natural athleticism, reactivity and reads, then you've got Marty Brodeur there with some of the greatest attributes to ever play the game. If you look at every goaltender, every one of those recipes is just a little different."

STYLE POINTS

It's difficult to find a predominant goaltending style in today's game. Saying "butterfly" would be the easiest, but it's almost become redundant because most goaltenders use a form of that style as part of their repertoire.

Some goalies are more patient before they commit to it than others, some will move around more on their skates before committing into it, whereas other guys will get down into it then move from their knees.

Using Clark's list of key attributes of an elite goaltender is a good jumping-off point to help define an individual's style. Each of the attributes is a sliding scale, and no two goalies really hit the same points and have the same mix of those scales.

"That's what makes it fascinating. There is no default as much as the default is the butterfly. There's no one way to play this position, no absolute rights or wrongs," says Kevin Woodley of *InGoal* magazine and NHL.com. "That's what fascinates me the most about goaltending. It's all sorts of varying degrees of different systems, styles, save executions, strengths, weaknesses, and preferences. There really is no absolute to any of it."

In today's game, Woodley points to Nashville's Juuse Saros as an example of a goaltender who uses every tool in his toolbox to be successful in the current style of play.

Saros played in a league-leading 67 games for the Predators in 2021–22, going 38–25–3 with a .918 save percentage and 2.64 goals against average. Smallish in stature for today's goaltender at just 5-foot-11 and 180 pounds, Saros finished third in Vezina Trophy voting behind Shesterkin and Markstrom, now with Calgary.

"Saros is not six feet tall and sort of manages to succeed with speed, efficiency and patience on his skates, more than other goalies who are a lot bigger and rely more on their size," Woodley explains. "It's just comes back to that sliding scale for every guy, every body type, every athletic ability, every skating ability.

"But there is one sort of common denominator to all of it. As the game becomes increasingly east west from an attack standpoint, if you can't move, you can't play. An ability to beat plays on your skates and not commit early to the butterfly is a skill that is increasingly required against that style of attack."

TECH TALK

A term that gets thrown around a lot when describing goalies is *technical*. This has nothing to do with something specific. It basically means that a goalie uses their skill set to be in the right place at the right time.

Watching a technical goaltender, you'd see somebody who moves with efficiency, and goes in and out of their posts with a plan that is executed on a consistent basis. Post plays is so incredibly important in today's game because so much of the attack is funneled out of the corners and behind the net and from bad angles. It's not just about being able to cover your posts and seal your post, it's about being able to move in and out of it.

In addition, a good technical goaltender rarely chases the play, doesn't get caught swimming in his crease, and is able to move from the butterfly in an efficient manner.

There are a few goalies that have taken the technical aspect to another level. A goalie is expected to be able to cover the ice on their knees, but Shesterkin and Andrei Vasilevskiy are two current examples of goalies that move as well on their knees as most goalies used to be on their skates.

All of these technical elements need to be part of the game plan that a goalie can execute consistently. There's the technical element in terms of the movement patterns, and also being able to execute them efficiently.

There's also the tactical side of being able to know where you are on the ice at any given moment. This aspect of being technical needs to be part of a set plan and system that doesn't vary, as opposed to a goalie who comes out of the crease and plays with a lot of backwards flow as the play moves in on them. At that point they are freelancing a bit with too many moving parts to hinder proper execution.

At the NHL level, Woodley says a goalie needs to be more than just technically sound to be successful.

"The one thing I'd say though, I'm not sure being good technically is enough anymore. Those foundational pieces of goaltending are being taught to so many from such a young age. I think you have to have more than that in order to separate yourself at this level. I don't know that anyone gets away with just being a really good technical goaltender. You need more than just consistency to thrive in the NHL. Now you need another layer on top of that."

THE NEXT LAYER

Finding that next layer isn't as simple as it sounds. Just like Clark's recipe for an elite goaltender, the measurements of the ingredients can vary from person to person.

For some guys, it's the ability to read and anticipate the play. For other guys, it's athleticism in the form of speed and how they compete or battle. It could also be that instinctive ability in a crazy moment to go outside the box and come up with a creative way to make a save that they maybe haven't done before.

Being based in Vancouver, Woodley spends a lot of his time covering Canucks goaltender Thatcher Demko. Over the course of his career, Demko has added that instinctive element to his game, making scorpion-like saves to go along with his excellent technique and consistent tactics that have made him one of the league's top netminders.

Woodley says that Demko's ability to work with Clark and add that layer to his game was essential in his growth and development.

"The game of hockey is just too dynamic and too unpredictable to always be perfect. So what do you do in those moments when the game's no longer perfect? Can you find an answer? Outside of all the things that you've rehearsed, can you be creative? Can you show that instinct? These are the questions a goalie needs to think about when adding that layer to help separate them from the pack."

SIZING THEM UP

The issue of size has been a hot-button topic with goaltenders, especially in recent years. For most evaluators, the taller a goalie is, the better prospect he'll be. Woodley says it's a very real thing that some teams won't even consider drafting a goalie if they are under 6-foot 2.

That's why it's refreshing to see what Saros is doing with Nashville. What he lacks in inches, he more than makes up for with his poise and athleticism. He definitely gives hope to others of his size, and it should also make scouts think twice about shutting the door.

There's also Jonathan Bernier, who has played more than 400 games with six different teams over his 10-year career. He may not have totally matched the expectations from his draft projections, but he's gone on to carve a pretty good career for a guy who is just six feet tall. If his draft was held today, there's a probably a very real chance he wouldn't even be selected.

To overcome that perceived lack of size, a goalie needs to more patient on their skates like Saros, have exceptional skating ability, and make sure to never be playing from behind. It's about doing whatever it takes to overcome that lack of square footage coverage to take up a little more ice and still be able to recover from it effectively.

"If you're 5-foot-11 or 6-foot tall, it doesn't mean you can't play. I just think we have gotten to the point where the big ones get a lot of chances, and the little ones don't get nearly enough," says Woodley.

"And rather than looking at it and saying either guy can succeed, to many it just looks different. There's less margin for error when you're smaller, because pucks are just going to hit you. But at a certain point, there's also impediments to being big that you have to overcome as well."

SWEET SPOT

In his conversations with people around the hockey world, Woodley has determined that the ideal size for a goaltender in the current NHL is about 6-foot-3. As one goalie coach explained to Woodley, on either side of that scale you have to overcome your size.

So the guy who is three inches taller than that at 6-foot-6, that's a big body that has long legs that have to get to the ice. Along with long legs that you have to lean back over top of to seal the short side posts. Not to mention the holes that open up when moving east to west just because of the nature of the frame. There are a lot of moving parts that Woodley says some taller goalies have difficulty dealing with.

"It takes a whole lot more power to get that big frame moving. If I'm on my knees and I need to move to my left, I have to lift my right leg up off the ice until I can catch an edge to make that push. The longer those levers are, the higher I have to raise that knee off the ice before I establish that edge and push. And that opens up a bigger hole because it takes longer to do. So you have to generate a good edge and load it a little bit more. And those are all holes that get opened, along with delays in movements. It becomes an impediment you have to overcome at a certain size.

With the exception of guys like Markstrom (6-foot-6 and Jake Oettinger (6-foot-5), much of Woodley's theory does hold water with the current crop of elite NHL goalies.

Andrei Vasilevskiy and Ville Husso both check in at 6-foot-3, Binnington and Sergei Bobrovsky are both 6-foot-2, while Shesterkin and Jonathan Quick are 6-foot-1.

Both guys on either side of the height scale have to overcome size in different manners. The difference is the 6-foot-6 kid is going to get every opportunity to play, but the 6-footer probably won't have nearly as much margin for error. Most of them won't even get a shot.

STAY ON TRACK

As the shooters continue to do whatever it takes to improve their techniques, goalies are doing their best to keep up. However, it's not always about getting stronger and faster.

The mechanics of tracking have now become a point of emphasis for many goalies in their daily training routines. Woodley says it's actually quite misunderstood in the mainstream because people just haven't taken the time to understand what it actually involves.

Some will say that tracking is just looking at the puck and goalies have been doing that forever. To a certain extent, that's right. But using the new biomechanics, this version of tracking is not just about how a goalie looks at the puck, it's also about how they set up their posture and move their head in order to look at the puck.

In the scientific studies that have been done with tracking, it comes down to the vestibular function and how the body reacts to head movement based on its perception of balance and binocular vision and how that plays into it.

Studies have shown there's a certain way to move your head to maximize your ability to see a puck off the release, and there's a certain way to move your head and movement that's going to decrease all those delays to set and square. Especially with the bigger goalies and the opening and the closing of the movements, this plays a role in decreasing those.

Woodley says that goalies of thirty to forty years ago played a much different style, almost like they were moving out of the way of shots and being forced to make dramatic windmill catches.

Using this method of tracking, goalies are being taught to recognize that they really don't have to worry about that six-by-four net behind them because that's a big space. But then in order to get to that net, there's a much smaller net in front of them that the puck has to go through. If they can think about closing that down in front of them rather than that giant thing behind them, it makes the game easier mentally.

"We've absolutely gotten scientific, whether it's angles or whether it's vestibular function and biomechanics. Goaltending movement is broken down much like a golf swing, to find peak efficiencies. For twenty-plus years, goalies spent every summer working on their skills—technical, position-specific skills. And all the players did for most of those twenty years was worry about becoming bigger, stronger, and faster. That's how they trained," Woodley explains.

"Well, that's kind of turned on it here a little bit and they finally caught up to the goaltending fraternity. Now, shooters are spending their summers working on skills—shooting coaches, deception, white ice techniques, and ways to make it look like you're shooting one place and get the goalie moving and then deliver it to a different area. Those are all sort of relatively new and goaltending has to sort of stay on top of and catch up."

Woodley believes the scales have definitely started to tip back towards the players to a degree, and now it's on the goalies to find an answer.

But in reality, the goaltending fraternity has never stopped looking for the answers. Woodley says that for as long as he can remember, NHL goalies would use their summer to go back to goalie school. And this wasn't just a way for them to stay in shape during the offseason.

"These were professional goaltenders literally going back to school to work on things like movement efficiency, proper leg recovery, post coverage, skills, and overall technique. The recognition and the importance of skill development is just something that goalies have always done."

DELAYED DEVELOPMENT

The road to becoming an NHL goaltender is often very windy and laden with numerous pot holes along the way. Of all the positions in hockey, Woodley says it's definitely the one that involves the most development.

"Goaltending is the one position that we're always told takes longer to develop. That doesn't have to be a blanket statement because it's definitely not true all the time. But we certainly see plenty of examples of guys who—drafted or undrafted—take a long time to get there.

"I've always thought that's because I just think sometimes it takes a while for a young guy to find the right voice to listen to. Sometimes you have guys bounce around multiple organizations, and all sudden, there'll be a coach or something they teach that's just a little different or just sort of speaks to them in a different way. Nobody's reinventing the wheel here, so maybe it's the approach from this person just connects better. But there's just something different that clicks with guys at different points."

A shining example of this is a goalie who made his NHL debut in 2021, more than eight years after being drafted.

Zach Fucale was living the dream in 2013. On May 26, he won a Memorial Cup championship with the Halifax Mooseheads on a team that featured future NHLers Jonathan Drouin and Nathan MacKinnon.

A few weeks later, Fucale was the top-ranked goaltender in the 2013 NHL Entry Draft, where he was selected by the Montreal in the second round.

Fucale seemed destined for immediate success. He played four seasons of junior hockey in QMJHL with Halifax (2011–14) and Quebec (2014–15), finishing with a career record of 134–49–14.

His stellar resume also featured success at the international level. Fucale twice represented Canada in the Under-20 World Junior Championship, winning gold in 2015 while posting an unblemished 5–0 record with two shutouts. This was Fucale's second gold medal for Canada, having also won an Under-18 title in 2012.

But Fucale's path to the NHL had a roadblock, and that road-block's name was Carey Price.

Price was in the middle of putting together a stellar NHL career that saw him win the Hart Trophy as league MVP in 2015 with a career-best 44 wins. There's no chance that Fucale was about to supplant the legendary Price from his crease, so he would bide his time in the AHL with Montreal's farm team, the St. John's Ice Caps.

One season became two, and then three, and so on. Fucale would eventually move on from the Canadiens organization, becoming a minor-league nomad with nine different teams over six seasons.

Fucale's minor-league journey rolled on to Hershey, Pennsylvania, after he signed a contract with Washington in 2020.

In his second season in the Capitals organization, Fucale finally got the call he'd been waiting his entire life for.

Fucale would play his first NHL game on November 11, 2021, exactly eight years, four months, and twelve days after hearing his name called at the 2013 draft.

Now 26 years and 167 days old, Fucale would make the most of his first career NHL start, stopping all twenty-one shots he faced in a 2–0 shutout of Detroit. In the process, he became the first Capitals goalie to record a shutout in the first NHL game.

"I can't dream it better, to be honest," Fucale told reporters after the game. "This is a really great moment. At the end of the day, it's a great win, and it's been a hell of a journey. But now one is out of the way, we move on and we go to the next game. That's the reality of it."

Fucale played two more games for the Capitals before being returned to Hershey. He finished the season with a record of 1–1–1, along with 1.75 goals against average and .924 save percentage. After the shutout in his debut, Fucale didn't allow a goal until the third period of his second game, setting an NHL record for longest shutout streak to start a career.

Woodley has paid close attention to Fucale throughout his career, especially his time in junior hockey. He says that Fucale's career has really come full circle, and he's doing things now that he wasn't doing early on. Woodley mentioned that Fucale had also reconnected with some coaches and advisers that he'd worked with previously back in juniors.

"There are a lot of different factors [that] go into that beyond just the pressure and expectations, especially in Montreal, along with all of the success he had at a young age. But then also, there's the issue of not only losing his way in the minors, but having different influences from different voices all trying to get him to do things a different way.

"It's only in the past, I'd say year and a half, that he's sort of rediscovered some of this different style of foundation. But again, I don't know that he should be pointed to as a total failure. And yet, based on the draft position, which was based on the success of the team, it's hard to argue anything else [except] that he was just drafted in the wrong spot."

TAKING RESPONSIBILITY

It may sound like an oversimplification to say that a new voice or approach will help crack the code for some players along the way; there also needs to be some personal responsibility involved.

Just like the teenager who thinks they know everything (I'm speaking from personal experience), an athlete needs to be willing to take advice and accept criticism. Just because you are doing something one way doesn't mean there isn't a better option available to you, or at least it's something to consider. By simply shutting out that input, you are limiting yourself to growth opportunities.

Whether it's warranted or not, some guys just aren't ready to listen to the advice that a particular coach has to offer them. Take Jacob Markstrom, for example.

For years, Markstrom was considered "the best goalie outside the NHL," but for some reason he couldn't make the jump. Part of that was there were flaws in his game, somewhat tied to his size.

With Markstrom's size and aggressive nature at the time, he needlessly moved around too much, got caught out of position, and opened up a ton of holes. Did the goalie coaches in Florida identify that at the time? Absolutely they did. But after hearing for all those years about how great he was, was Markstrom willing to make those changes? Not at that point, according to Woodley.

After making his NHL debut with Florida in January 2011, Markstrom was dealt to Vancouver in March 2014 in a four-player trade that saw Luongo sent to the Panthers.

Since arriving in western Canada, Markstrom has lived up to all the advance hype he carried as he entered the league as a brash twenty-one year-old, and is now among the NHL's elite goaltenders. He posted three straight seasons of 20 wins or more with Vancouver from 2017 to 2020.

Markstrom signed as a free agent with Calgary in 2020, won a career-high 37 games in 2021–22, and was the runner-up to Shesterkin for the Vezina Trophy.

Sometimes it takes a trade and another voice saying, "Hey, this has to change" before a player is willing to budge on their principles. Woodley has seen this play out all too often and says that players have to be willing to listen to all the voices around them to figure out their best path.

"I don't think it's as simple as saying goalies just take time to develop. Realistically they just aren't capable of developing any faster. There's a famous quote that says 'When the student is ready, the teacher will appear.' It doesn't matter if it's a goalie or a goal scorer. Sometimes a player just needs to connect with the right mentor, the right coach, or the right voice, at the right time."

Woodley has more recently witnessed a similar scenario play out in in Vancouver with 27-year-old goaltender Spencer Martin.

A third-round pick of Colorado in 2013, Martin landed in Vancouver as part of a three-team trade in July 2021.

Martin played three fairly nondescript NHL games with the Avs in 2016–17, going 0–2–1 with an .865 save percentage and goals against average of 4.65. One of the games was a 5–2 loss to San Jose, and Martin gave up five goals on just 26 shots.

Throughout his six minor league stops over a seven-year period in places like San Antonio, Syracuse, and Orlando, it was pretty typical of Martin to record a save percentage in the high eights and low nines, along with a goals against average somewhere in the threes.

Fast forward to 2021–22, and Martin suddenly turned into the second coming of Kirk McLean with the Canucks.

Martin was 19–4–2 with the AHL's Abbotsford Canucks, and was among the league leaders in shutouts (three), goals against average (2.43), and save percentage (.914).

More importantly, in six games of action with the big club in Vancouver, Martin recorded three wins, two shootout losses, and an overtime defeat where he stopped 47 of 50 shots in a 3–2 setback to Edmonton.

As for the other stats? How about a stingy 1.74 goals against average to go along with a tidy .950 save percentage?

It sounds like somebody was listening to goalie guru Ian Clark.

"After all those years of bouncing around, Martin made a few changes in training camp after arriving in Vancouver," Woodley says. "Then he made a few more tweaks during the season. Martin got a shot with the Canucks and he ran with it. Now he's signed to be probably the backup for the next few years."

Despite Martin's age, Canucks management also saw the potential in him and rewarded him for his hard work. In April 2022, Martin signed a two-year deal worth $1.525 million.

And it was all because he decided to listen to a new voice that belonged to Ian Clark.

6

FACEOFFS

For an event that takes place sixty to seventy times within a hockey game, it's extremely difficult to draw a straight line between faceoff success and team success. To be honest, it's almost impossible. Gurus have been analyzing faceoffs for years now, and even their final conclusions don't seem to make things any clearer.

Faceoffs can be very important in the moment, but difficult to decipher in the bigger picture. One of the reasons faceoffs get so much attention in the first place is because they take place at a stoppage in play. It's one of the few moments in a hockey game where both the players and fans can catch their breath. As opposed to a football game, where there's more downtime than there is actual game action.

It's also a chance for the broadcasters to use this pause in the action to conveniently throw in some faceoff stats to pump up the moment even more. In all the frenzied action of a hockey game, the moment of a faceoff sometimes gets more attention than it really deserves.

If you think about it, a faceoff is hockey's version of the pitcher versus batter moment in baseball. It's the one event in a game where the pause helps to create immediate conflict between two individuals.

Even the NHL is trying to capitalize on this moment with the introduction of "faceoff probability" data that made its television debut in 2022.

As part of the NHL's partnership with Amazon Web Services, more than ten years of historic faceoff data was thrown into a blender to come up with instant probability numbers for the two men stepping in to take the draw.

Once calculated, the stats are displayed on the broadcast, and can even be updated in real time if one of the players gets waved out of the circle for any reason.

"This data source was significantly varied and complex, incorporating such information as a player's home and away faceoff statistics, head-to-head matchup history, player characteristics such as height, weight, and handedness, and game context such as the faceoff location, game score, and faceoff time," explains Priya Ponnapalli, senior manager of Amazon Machine Learning Solutions Lab.

"This combination of historical success rates, player matchup characteristics, and game context brings together HITS and puck and player tracking data to provide a complete perspective for a faceoff's dynamics."

From a fan engagement standpoint, faceoff probability is exactly what hockey needs more of. They've created an easily digestible element of the broadcast by using the AWS technology and information that just creates more interest in the moment.

It doesn't add any more credibility to the faceoff, but it does help enhance the fan viewing experience. It could also be a good jumping-off point for in-game betting, although the window of time to place a faceoff bet seems to be awfully tight.

The argument of trying to correlate faceoffs with winning or losing is something Mike Kelly is all too familiar with. Kelly is the director of media and content for Sportlogiq, a Montreal-based sports analytics firm, and you've probably also seen his outstanding work on television as an analyst for the NHL Network.

Kelly has heard the analytics crowd crowing for years about the actual importance of faceoffs, and he has done his best to listen to both sides of the argument. But most importantly, Kelly is all for anything that helps open some more eyes to the game's statistical elements.

"Hockey is a very chaotic sport, and faceoffs are one of the few things that are controllable. It always starts the same way with a referee dropping a puck. But from there, it's complete chaos in terms of what happens on the ice; nobody knows what's going to happen next. So it's a logical starting point.

"And it's an entry point to get fans more engaged with real time, probabilities, and analytics. But there's great growth potential as well. And this is what we work with our broadcast partners on consistently. It's also what I focus on in the work I do in the media is, finding ways to provide insight and illumination into what's happening in the game to the fan in the least intrusive way possible."

TEAM STATS

By simply looking at a team's faceoff totals for the season, you'd have a difficult time figuring out who the good and bad teams are.

Florida claimed the Presidents' Trophy in 2021–22 as the team with the best regular season record, finishing 58–18–6 for 122 points. They also scored a league-best 340 goals and owned a record of 31–10–0 in games decided by three or more goals. All very impressive numbers, to say the least.

But Florida finished twenty-second in the league in faceoff percentage at 48.2, winning just 2,364 of 4,901 total faceoffs.

The top five teams in faceoff winning percentage were Toronto, Dallas, Boston, Carolina, and Los Angeles. In the overall NHL standings they finished fourth, fifteenth, tenth, third, and fourteenth respectively.

Of the teams in the bottom five in faceoff percentage, only one of them made the playoffs—Colorado, the eventual Stanley Cup champion.

The Avalanche didn't have much more faceoff success in the playoffs, ending the postseason ranked fourteenth of sixteen teams at 47.8 percent. Their opponent in the Final didn't fare much better either, as Tampa Bay wound up in tenth spot at 49 percent.

Remarkably, Colorado lost the faceoff battle in five of the six games against Tampa Bay with the other game deadlocked at 50 percent apiece.

FIVE-YEAR ANALYSIS

In the five seasons from 2017 to 2022, the five teams with the most total faceoff wins are: Dallas (11,606), Carolina (11,549), Nashville (11,548), Philadelphia (11,545), and Toronto (11,536).

Did having top-five faceoff numbers result in team success during these five seasons?

Dallas made the playoffs in three of the five seasons, going as far as the Stanley Cup Final in 2020, where they lost to Tampa Bay in the Edmonton bubble.

Carolina has been to the postseason four times in this span, but they came up short against Boston in the 2019 Eastern Conference finals.

It's been a good five-year run for Nashville, qualifying for the playoffs in all five seasons. Yet they've only been able to get past the first round once.

Philadelphia has only made the postseason twice during this time, with their most recent success being a first-round win over Montreal in 2020.

As for the Maple Leafs, they were a playoff team in each of these five seasons. But we all know how these seasons ended. The Maple Leafs have been eliminated in the first round for six straight seasons, and haven't won a playoff series since 2004. (How long has that been? My daughter turned two that summer. She's now a junior in college.)

Faceoff wins may look good on the stat sheet, but they definitely aren't a harbinger of success and certainly don't guarantee a Stanley Cup.

SOMETHING IS BRUIN

Without question, Boston center Patrice Bergeron has been the gold standard for faceoff excellence in the NHL for nearly two decades. Bergeron's 991 faceoff wins in 2021–22 led the league for the seventh time in his career, while also posting the highest winning percentage at 61.9.

Bergeron made his NHL debut in 2003–04, and his career totals over the last 17 seasons are all at or near the top of the league's faceoff categories.

Bergeron's 24,500 total faceoffs are 323 more than that of Sidney Crosby, and 2,000 ahead of that of third-place Anze Kopitar. With 14,139 wins, Bergeron's closest competitor is Crosby at 12,580. Among the four players with more than 20,000 draws (Bergeron, Crosby, Kopitar, and Eric Staal), Bergeron's winning percentage of 57.1 is more than 5 percent higher than that of Crosby.

Bergeron's work on the penalty kill is also without peer. His 3,319 total draws taken in shorthanded situations give him a sizable lead over both Ryan Kesler (2,993) and Tomas Plekanec (2,705). With a winning percentage, of 51.5, Bergeron also leads the league with 1,709 shorthanded wins.

Furthering his reputation as the NHL's best two-way forward, Bergeron has been awarded the Selke Trophy a record five times in his career. The Selke recognizes "the forward who best excels in the defensive aspects of the game," and Bergeron has now been a finalist for 11 consecutive seasons. This surpasses Wayne Gretzky's ten-year run of being a finalist for the Hart Trophy as NHL MVP from 1980 to 1989.

At even strength, Bergeron's 17,663 faceoffs are second only to Crosby's 18,183. However, Bergeron edges out Sid for the top spot in wins by a count of 10,377 to 9,312.

Bergeron also gets a considerable amount of time on the power play in Boston, and his 3,518 total faceoffs and 2,053 wins both rank him fourth overall.

Remarkably, Bergeron's rookie campaign in 2003–04 was the only season he finished below 50 percent in overall winning percentage. He's had five seasons of 60 percent or better over the last 17 years and has won the Selke Trophy in three of those seasons. Bergeron's single-season high in winning percentage is 62.25 in 2020–21.

During a period from 2000 to 2008, forward Yanic Perreault had an incredible five seasons where he blew past 60 percent in winning percentage, including a gaudy 65.2 percent (561–300) in 2003–04 in 69 games with Montreal.

THAT'S MOORE LIKE IT

Having spent the majority of his 13-year NHL career in the Eastern Conference, Dominic Moore knows all too well what it's like to square off against Bergeron in the faceoff circle.

"It's no secret that Bergeron was always tough on me. It's pretty easy to see why he's always been at the very top of his game. He's just so strong and his timing is always so quick," Moore explains. "You kind of knew what he was going to do, but it didn't necessarily mean you were going to be able stop it. As the centerman and the faceoff guy, I always looked forward to facing guys like him. But you always know you're going to have a long night ahead of you with lots of tough faceoff battles."

Moore suited up for ten different teams between 2003 and 2018, playing the majority of his 897 career games with the New York Rangers, Toronto, and Tampa Bay.

No slouch on the draw himself, Moore has a career faceoff win percentage of 53.3 percent, with a record of 5,041 wins and 4,416 losses. He was lethal on power plays at 59.9 percent (235–157) and owns a career record of 3,939–3,262 for 54.7 percent at even strength.

Moore's single-season high in wins was 665 in 2008–09 with Toronto and Buffalo, and he set his career-best winning percentage of 55.3 with the Rangers in 2015–16.

A graduate of Harvard University, Moore has always been a student of the game. He enjoys the analytical side of things and has naturally gotten involved in the faceoff discourse over the years.

Understanding firsthand that faceoff success often goes hand in hand with positive puck possession numbers, Moore is quick to offer his unique viewpoint.

"It's just another example of the analytics movement saying that faceoffs don't matter. And by no means is it the entire analytics movement. It's just a lot of people within that realm that like to bring this up all the time," says Moore, who now works as an analyst for ESPN's NHL coverage. "There are a lot of draws that happen throughout a game and most of them ended up around 50-50. So at the end of the game, then sure, maybe it doesn't matter.

"But they only don't matter until they do. It clearly does. And we know it does when we focus so much of our time discussing puck possession and all the stats that go along with that. If faceoffs are a frequent determiner of possession, then yes, we know it matters."

EXCELLENCE OF EXECUTION

While it may be difficult to connect the dots between faceoff stats and game results, there's no denying the effect they can have on certain situations in a game.

Think about an offensive zone draw late in the game for a team trailing by a goal. They could be getting smoked in the faceoff battle up until that point, but this one draw could be the difference between two points or none at all.

Win the draw cleanly and suddenly the team will look to create a scoring opportunity. But if the defense wins it, they need to decide how to get the puck out of the zone. Do they risk ringing it around the boards and potentially icing the puck, or are they able to skate the zone and chip it out? There are so many variables coming out of one simple faceoff.

Like Moore says, they don't matter until they do.

As the centerman in this situation, Moore says it was his job to evaluate the entire scenario even before he left the bench and make sure they executed it properly.

"It's the job of every player to know what they need to do and where they need to be. But at the end of the day, the center does feel a little bit like the quarterback walking up to the line of scrimmage.

You definitely need to be aware of where the opposition is setting up, especially for defensive zone draw. By looking at that you might know what type of shot they are trying to set up, or what play they might be looking to run.

"Teams are always watching video of each other to see what types of set plays are being run off a faceoff, so we need to be ready for that. We don't have that many set plays in hockey, unlike football where it's essentially a game full of set plays. Faceoffs are one of the areas in hockey where a team can run a set play, so there's a lot of X's and O's being drawn up on the whiteboard during a game."

STAT FINDINGS

Isolating faceoff outcomes in certain scenarios was the goal of a presentation made at the 2019 MIT Sloan Sports Analytics Conference in Boston.

Each year, the leading figures in sports analytics, business, and technology gather in Beantown for two days to discuss and debate the ongoing confluence of statistics and sports. (Moore was part of a panel at the 2022 summit that bantered about the growth of analytics in the NHL.)

At the thirteenth annual conference, a presentation titled "Winning Isn't Everything: A Contextual Analysis of Hockey Face-offs" was made by Nick Czuzoj-Shulman and his staffers from Sportlogiq. The group did an in-depth study on more than 71,000 faceoffs that took place during the 2017–18 NHL season.

Instead of simply trying to affix faceoff percentages to team wins, the group focused their efforts on studying the effects of faceoffs in specific situations.

In all the data that was mined for the research project, the group came to the conclusion that there was value in winning faceoffs cleanly in the offensive zone and directing pucks to high-danger areas.

The study stated: "When a player wins the draw cleanly, his team can execute drawn-up set plays with greater ease and will therefore have better chances of catching the defending team off-guard or out of position."

Sportlogiq's in-depth analysis determined that a clean win in the offensive zone resulted in a shot on goal or scoring chance 38.6 percent of the time. For non-clean wins, it was 30.3 percent. A clean win that was directed back and to the inside of the faceoff circle led to shot attempts 43.6 percent of the time, while it was 32.1 percent for non-clean wins.

Drilling down even deeper, clean wins were also sent to a teammate's stick 25 percent quicker than non-clean wins were.

The group also detailed the numerous variables or questions that can affect the outcome of offensive zone faceoffs. These included the side of the ice where the faceoff took place, was the player taking the draw left- or right-handed, was the win clean, and where was the puck directed.

PREP TIME

There's no question that players take pride in having success on faceoffs. Because of the spotlight placed on each one, a considerable amount of preparation goes into being one of the best at the craft.

On the day before a game, the team's video coach will typically prepare a collection of clips to show the centers what they might be able to expect from the counterparts on the next opponent.

The video will include various faceoffs from both the offensive and defensive zones. Even if they've gone up against a player multiple times in their career, this will give them a look at what tendencies that player is currently leaning towards.

While watching the video, Moore compares it to doing a general pre-scout of a team. Not only is he watching to see what his opponent's tendencies might be, he's also trying to get a better look at what they do well and what potentially might work against them. Then it becomes a matter of incorporating all of this information into how he normally approaches each draw.

At the morning skate, it's not unusual to see one of the coaches working with the centers, using the video to help reinforce what could be expected that night. It's also a way for the centers to work on their timing, although that's not a perfect scenario either because the pucks aren't being dropped by a linesman like they are in a game.

Even if just one or two extra wins come as a result of the practice and remedial video work, it could wind up being the difference-maker in a game.

"I think faceoffs are like anything in life. If you care about it, then you'll put the time in to become successful at it. That's how I've always approached things. Even going back to college hockey, I'd always strive to be as complete player as I possibly could," says Moore.

"I was the type of player that didn't want to have any weaknesses. And knowing how centers are such an important part of the game, I just always wanted to continually get better at faceoffs. If it meant extra practice, watching video, and pre-scouting the opponent, it's a matter of just incorporating any possible way to get better."

BAG OF TRICKS

Life in the faceoff circle is about as unpredictable as it gets in the game of hockey. No two players are really alike, and the same goes for the linesmen dropping the puck. This isn't a puck being dropped by a mechanical device with precise timing. A fraction of a second can make a huge difference in a how a player reacts to the puck being dropped.

It's not much different than trying to predict what the opponent is about to do. Every good faceoff artist has a bag of tricks loaded with surprises. Some players live and die by just being powerful, while others are more about working angles and technique with footwork and leverage.

By showing different looks and being unpredictable, a good centerman will make it very difficult for the opposition to have any kind of success regardless of what the game situation is.

Bergeron is the perfect example of someone who befuddles the opposition with his arsenal of attack methods. On one draw he's simply overpowering you with his strength. The next time he might lunge into the circle and take you by surprise, or he might simply drop down and wait for help from one of his wingers on a 50-50 draw. It's that kind of element of surprise that has made him so dominant in the role for so long.

With so much going on in the moment, Moore says he himself was never the type of player to overthink a faceoff scenario with things like different hand positioning depending on the location of the draw, and worrying about how he was going to get his feet set beforehand. He was more concerned about ensuring success with a solid plan.

It was about immediately taking stock of the situation and making sure everyone around him was on the same page. For Moore, it was all about doing whatever it took for him to have the best odds at winning the draw cleanly, and not losing it cleanly.

"It never really changed for me from draw to draw. Again, it all comes down to maximizing your odds of success with every draw, and doing your job in a way that makes you comfortable. First and foremost for me it was understanding who I was going up against and trying to figure out what they are trying to do in that situation. From the moment I got off the bench, I was computing a ton of information in my head.

"Almost like a computer, at some point I'd spit out a final result in my head of what my approach was going to be. But that came after carefully taking a lot of factors into consideration—the score of the game, whether the guy I was facing was left- or right-handed, what zone were we in, what side of the ice is it, time left in the game, who were my linemates, and who were we going up against. It's like I was doing an analytics calculation on the fly with just seconds to prepare for it, trying to figure out my best odds for success.

"And then I'd get kicked out of the draw and realize I'd wasted all that time for nothing," jokes Moore.

FINAL FORECAST

In his current role with ESPN, the 42-year-old Moore knows he now has a platform to share his unique insight into what he feels is an overlooked element of hockey. He understands the constant faceoff adjustments that are being made by the good players over the course of those chaotic 60 minutes.

It's those subtle game-within-a-game moments that maybe even the most ardent of fans can't appreciate or even notice at times.

The haters will always say there are so many faceoffs in a game that it's impossible to quantify their overall impact. It's even hard to justify success on a faceoff when someone that only wins 50 percent of the time is considered among the best at what they do. (Although, failing seven out of ten times when trying to hit a baseball is supposed to be the high-water mark for MLB success.)

But when that one faceoff decides the outcome of a game, it becomes a different story.

And just because the Colorado Avalanche were less than average on faceoffs when they won a Stanley Cup in 2022, it doesn't make them a bad team. Ten years from now, do you think anyone will even ask what their faceoff numbers were in the Finals?

Nevertheless, when looking at the big picture, Moore knows in his heart that faceoffs matter, even if the underlying numbers don't immediately bear it out.

So what does he tell the people who constantly come at him with the analytical mumbo jumbo about what is supposed to matter?

"Faceoffs are just like the weather. It could be sunny all week and you aren't even thinking about the rain. But if it rains on your wedding day, then suddenly it matters."

Like Moore says, they don't matter until they do.

7

IN-GAME STRATEGIES

Getting ready for a game is a never-ending cycle of preparation for an NHL coach. Whether it's on the team charter after a game headed for the next city, or an early arrival at the rink before a morning skate or practice, their job is to make sure the players have all the information they need for their next opponent.

Someone that knows all about this grind is Dave Barr, a hard-nosed forward who collected 332 points during a solid 13-year NHL career with Boston, New York Rangers, St. Louis, Hartford, Detroit, New Jersey, and Dallas.

"They're so busy in the NHL, playing three games or more each week. You finish a game on a Tuesday, then you're flying overnight to play somewhere else on Wednesday. We're on the plane reviewing the last game and preparing for the next one at the same time."

With his playing days in the rearview mirror, Barr has since served as an assistant coach with six teams over twelve years: San Jose (2017–19), Florida (2016–17), Buffalo (2015–16), New Jersey (2011–14), Minnesota (2009–11), and Colorado (2008–09).

Barr also led Canada to a gold medal at the 2021 U-18 World Championships and has won titles in both the American Hockey League and Ontario Hockey League. Most recently he served as the head coach of the Vienna Capitals in the Austrian ICE Hockey League in 2021–22.

Regardless of the situations he's been in over the years, Barr always emphasized communication with the players. The overload of information can be overwhelming, especially with younger players still trying to find their way. But at the end of the day, everyone has a job to do and it's always about trying to win a hockey game.

"When we meet with the players in the morning of a game, we'll go over video of the power play and penalty kill that the other team is going to utilize. We might also show some clips of how they transition through the neutral zone. If we've played them before, we review what happened the last time, looking back at what worked and what didn't.

"There's also some individual meetings if you're trying [to] get a specific message through to certain players. It's definitely a lot of information and it's all explained to them fairly quickly."

One of the things that Barr focused on heavily during his various stops was special teams. He coordinated the penalty-killing units under head coach Peter DeBoer during his stints in both New Jersey and San Jose, and ran the power play in Minnesota.

DeBoer understood the value that Barr brought to the team and went out of his to recognize his contributions at morning skate in Toronto on January 4, 2018, when he was asked to explain the success of San Jose's penalty killing at the time.

"We ran a penalty kill in New Jersey when I had Dave Barr on my staff there. We were number one in the league, and I think we had a modern-day record for penalty-kill percentage in a season the year we went to the Stanley Cup Final in 2012. After I moved on we went with some different philosophies. We kind of got away from what we were doing there, and just thought the game was changing.

"I rehired Dave and we went back to that, and I think that's made a big difference. He's done a great job implementing it. It just goes to show you that sometimes you can overthink things. Every season, everyone talks about how the game's changed. A lot of things may change, but a lot of things may still apply and a lot of the principles will apply. It was just a matter of us reinstituting those."

DeBoer was correct about Barr coaching up success on the penalty kill in New Jersey, as the 2011–12 Devils set a modern-day record for penalty-killing efficiency. In fact, the record still stands today.

New Jersey killed off 232 of 259 shorthanded situations for a league-best percentage of 89.6, breaking the previous record of 89.3 percent set by Dallas during the 1999–2000 season. The 27 power play goals allowed by New Jersey that season were the fewest in the league, six less than Pittsburgh.

Barr brought that shorthanded wisdom with him to San Jose, piloting them to the league's second-best penalty killing unit in 2017–18 at 84.8 percent. The Sharks allowed a league-low 34 power play goals against on 224 opportunities, five fewer than Los Angeles.

Unfortunately, Barr was part of the purge when San Jose fired DeBoer and his entire coaching staff in December 2019. But Barr was hardly to blame for the demise, as the Sharks owned the league's top penalty-killing percentage at the time.

SETTING THE BARR

I had the chance to sit down with Dave in April of 2022, and we discussed numerous topics and situations that coaches have to deal with during a game.

If you feel like you're having a successful night of bench management, what is going right for you on those occasions?

"That's a loaded question because everybody has their own idea of what bench management means to them. Some coaches put a real emphasis on matching lines with certain players or lines. If you're playing against [Niklas]Backstrom, Ovechkin, and who's ever playing the wing with those two, you might decide that you want a particular matchup with them all night long. So before the game you'll say 'Hey, we're gonna match up the Smith line against the Backstrom line. So if you see them on the ice, as soon as you can get a change that makes sense, please let's try to get this accomplished.' This is especially important when you're on the road and you don't have last change. Some coaches are real matchup guys, so it's real important to them to emphasize this. That's one way of managing your players.

"I think another big part of it is recognizing when somebody's having an off game and recognizing when somebody's having a good game. I don't know if I've ever seen [a] guy play poorly for two and a half periods and then suddenly play really well the last 10 minutes of a game. It just doesn't happen, and sometimes we as coaches don't recognize it. Yes, my best right winger is having an off night tonight but I'm going to keep playing him to get through it; maybe he'll find it soon. I think that's important.

"It's also really important to recognize when certain players are playing well and are on top of their game for whatever reason. If you notice that someone is a little tired and they just don't have it, then maybe it's time to shuffle the lines to get some jump. This is [an] important part because you can make a big difference by pulling a guy up from the fourth line who's doing his job and has the capabilities of playing on the second or third line. So you move him up and now he's got some spark on the second or the third line, which buoys them. Recognizing when players are on their game is a big part of game management."

If your best player only has two shots through two periods and just looks off, as opposed to a fourth-line player who you can almost tell from the first shift that he's not having a good night, would you give that first line player a little more rope?

"For sure. I don't know if there's one coach who wouldn't do that. You have to show confidence in your guys. And it's really the reason why they're playing on the top couple of forward lines in the first place. They've shown that they can they can consistently create offense, make plays, and shoot the puck in the net. And, you know, sometimes they're not going to be on their game. I wouldn't be doing my job properly if I didn't talk to them about it, but there's a time and place for that. Maybe it's after the game or at practice the next morning.

"I might simply ask them how they felt about the previous game. Typically, they know it wasn't their best effort, so you try to talk through it with them and try to figure out why. It's definitely a very fine line about how you handle players on the top two lines. Even when they aren't in the zone, they still might be a better option than a third or fourth line guy brought up into that role. It really depends on the depth of your roster. But for the most part, you always give quite a bit of rope to your top guys."

What happens if you have pre-scouted the opposing team, but as the game goes on, they are doing things differently than you had planned for? Maybe they are running a different power play formation, or they are breaking out of their zone unlike they have in previous games. How do you go about suddenly making an in-game adjustment?

"For the most part everybody's systems are fairly close. They may have some points of difference, but they're fairly close. In most cases if the other team is doing something that's working really well in a game, usually it's us not doing our part correctly more than it is them doing something different. It could be something as simple as us making bad dump-in so that F1 [the first forward to enter the offensive zone] is not in a good position to put much pressure on their defenseman. Once you get into a game, it's usually more of an emphasis on what you need to be doing differently.

"When it comes to the power play, every team typically has about three breakouts they'll use a lot, and then they'll sprinkle in a fourth and a fifth one depending on who they're playing. If you are coaching the PK, you've already reminded your guys about their usual breakouts and plan for that. But then they might pull out one of those fourth or fifth ones and got a good scoring chance off the rush with one of those. Then you've gotta go to your PK guys and make them aware of what just happened and how we need to adjust. That might even be an on-bench adjustment that you make right away for the second half of that power play. A lot of times, that would be called down to the bench coaches from the coach in the press box. Most of the time, they've already recognized it, but you know, it's as simple as 'Hey, did you see what they did there? . . . Yeah, got it, thank you.'

"Most adjustments are made by the coaches during the intermission, maybe emphasizing what we're not doing as well as we need to do against this system. It's more about getting back to us doing what we need to do to be successful."

What is going on in the conversations we see on the bench during games between players and coaches?

"There's give and take, but I would say it's a little bit more of the coach talking to the players. The assistants usually talk to the players more than the head coach does. Sometimes you'll be talking to a player on the bench, and then another player comes off the ice and asks, 'What should I have done there?' Meanwhile, we haven't even seen the play because we were talking to the other guy. It's kind of funny, because a lot of times you just say, 'I was talking to someone else and didn't even see it, so tell me what happened.' Then they'll maybe describe it to you.

"Sometimes it might just be an effort thing, so you remind them of something they did on an earlier shift that worked well for them. 'Remember that exact same play in the first period when you lifted his stick and got body position? Look at the difference. You got the puck back and now we're leaving our defensive zone just because of that.'

"It's mostly about giving them a lot of positive feedback about what they're doing. But you also have to teach and explain that by not lifting his stick, they were able to control the puck and create a scoring chance.

"Most of the interaction with players comes from the assistant coaches. A lot of time the head coach will whisper to the assistant, 'Can you please talk to him about that?' Generally, the assistant coaches are the ones doing the teaching during games. And it's really teaching, as much as it is reminding guys what was talked about before the game and in the video room.

Have you noticed a change in how lines are constructed in recent years? Many teams are now nine deep on forward and the fourth line is expected to be more involved, especially in special team situations.

"You don't want to overplay your top guys, so in a perfect world your third and fourth line will each have a couple of guys that can play PK along with a reliable guy who can win faceoffs. That's a little bit why the fourth line has changed. You can't just have a tough guy that plays six shifts a game buried there. You can't afford that now with the speed and physicality of the game.

"With the demand of playing 82 games, you're expecting your top players to play 18 to 22 minutes a night. Everybody needs to contribute in some form. The NHL schedule is kind of a sprint to some degree. You can't suddenly run a marathon and decide not to use certain guys every night. You're trying to win every game."

THE LONG CHANGE

One of the things in games that often gets forgotten about is the long change that occurs during the second period, when each team's team bench is further away from the defensive zone. Players that get caught in the defensive zone for an extended period of time have an incredibly difficult time getting off the ice for a line change.

To make it worse, they just can't ice the puck to stop the play, because the offending team isn't allowed to make a line change. While the exhausted players may get a brief respite, they are stuck on the ice sucking wind while the other team has typically sent fresh troops out for the next shift.

If you ever see the time on ice charts after a game, it will be easy to spot the shifts where this has occurred, as some players can get stuck out there for two to three minutes at a time.

As a coach, how do you deal with the long change in the second period?

"It's funny because I bet that almost all of the coaches in the NHL remind their players about the long change every game during their first intermission talk. Typically what you do is instruct the winger who's farthest away from the bench that they may have to hang in there longer than usual if a change can't happen. They might have to stay out there a little bit longer so they'll just need to guard that side. Because normally the farthest ice away from the benches, that is the most dangerous. So he'll hang out, hang in there.

"And then a lot of times just one defenseman might change, normally the one closest to the bench side. Then the D who was on the far side will slide over to the strong side and the guy who comes on the ice goes on the ice and plays that far side positioning. So even though a right shot defenseman is coming to the bench and a left defenseman jumps on the ice, it's a little easier to change your left defenseman, who's remaining on the ice to play right defense until he has a chance to change. That's almost an automatic with every team. That's how you've tried to defend it. And then you know, big part of his where he put the puck and you know, where you dump the puck."

1, 2, 3, 4, 5 . . . 6?

According to morehockeystats.com, too many men on the ice penalties account for 90 percent of the bench minors assessed each season. It's considered by many to be an effective gauge of a coach's bench management skills, while others just write it off to overeager players and bad timing.

Too many men on the ice is designated as Rule 74.1 in the NHL rulebook, and is defined as follows: "Players may be changed at any time during the play from the players' bench provided that the player or players leaving the ice shall be within five feet of his players' bench and out of the play before the change is made. Refer also to Rule 71 – Premature Substitution. At the discretion of the on-ice officials, should a substituting player come onto the ice before his teammate is within the five foot limit of the players' bench (and therefore clearly causing his team to have too many players on the ice), then a bench minor penalty may be assessed."

It's that referee's discretion that led to all the hoopla surrounding Nazem Kadri's controversial overtime game-winner against Tampa Bay in Game 4 of the 2022 Stanley Cup Final. Kadri appeared to enter the play early before his teammate Nathan MacKinnon could get to the safe zone at the Avalanche bench.

Toronto led the league with 14 too many men on the ice minor penalties in 89 combined regular season and playoff games in 2021–22. Following close behind were Carolina (13 in 96 games), Calgary (13 in 94 games), and Tampa Bay (12 in 104 games).

Columbus was the league's smartest team on line changes, getting dinged for just two bench minors in 82 games. Buffalo, Dallas, and Detroit each had three.

On the ensuing power play, Carolina's five goals allowed were the most in the league. Nashville's penalties resulted in four goals, with Toronto and Tampa Bay each allowing three.

Since the 2015–16 season, six coaches have been behind the bench for 50 or more too many men on the ice minors. Here's a list of each coach with their total/games, and the number of goals allowed during the power play: Cooper (63/643, 13), Laviolette (61/573, 12), DeBoer (59/620, eight), Bednar (58/516, six), Blashill (51/542, eight), and John Hynes (50/539, 13).

In the case of a too many men on the ice penalty, who's more at fault—the coaches or players?

"I would say 80 percent of the time it's the player's fault. Sometimes we screw up, or the coaches will make a mistake. But most of the time it's the player's mistake.

"Normally when you get about halfway through a shift, the coach has already said who's up and a lot of times the assistant coach will be reminding them "Hey, Smith—[Mitch]Marner is right wing. That's your guy." So you'll be reminding Smith to start watching Marner if it looks like he's headed off.

"But what happens is just when you think a guy is coming to the bench, he's pretty close, you're amped up and you hop the boards to time the change—and suddenly Marner makes a right turn away from the bench to chase the puck. So it's a little bit of both guys' fault. The player on the bench isn't watching his player finish the shift, and the next thing you know he gets involved in a rush and there are six skaters on the ice. Typically it's because the two players involved in the change aren't on the same page."

EMPTY NETTER

Pulling the goalie late in the game can result in a couple of scenarios. The team that adds the extra attacker can tie the game to send it into overtime, or the team with the lead can add to their goal total by burying the puck into the empty net.

A quartet of teams each scored 21 empty net goals in 2021–22, led by Calgary's efficiency of 21 goals in 31 (61.3 percent) empty net opportunities. Also in the 21 club were St. Louis, Pittsburgh, and Edmonton.

On an individual basis, Washington's ageless wonder Alex Ovechkin led all skaters by scoring nine of his 50 into the yawning cage. Connor McDavid and Andrei Svechnikov each buried seven empty net goals, and a quartet of players were lurking close behind with six apiece.

Naturally, this a direct reflection of how many times a team was ahead late in the game and the opposition pulled their goalie for the extra skater.

In fact, the bottom eight teams in empty net goals scored were all non-playoff clubs: Philadelphia (six), Anaheim (eight), Chicago (eight), New Jersey (eight), Montreal (nine), New York Islanders (nine), San Jose (ten), and Arizona (ten).

That same logic applies to the teams that allowed the most empty net goals, showing how often they were trailing late in the game. Philadelphia gave up a league-high 27 empty netters, followed by Seattle (26), Detroit (26), and San Jose (23).

When it came to scoring with the extra attacker, Minnesota was by far the most successful team in the league with 21 goals, obliterating the previous record of 13 held by Toronto (2015–16) and Philadelphia (2016–17). The Wild scored 19 goals while playing six-on-five, and two at six-on-four.

The late-game heroics resulted in 12 standings points for Minnesota as they turned their empty-net prowess into five wins and a pair of shootout losses.

It used to be that teams trying to come back in a game with a late goal weren't pulling their goaltender until it was under two minutes remaining. Now it's happening with anywhere from three to five minutes left. Is there an explanation for the change?

"This is definitely one of the coaching decisions that analytics has become involved with. The numbers are now saying the farther out you pull the goalie, the better chance you have to tie the game or just score a goal. So coaches are now looking to get the extra attacker out there with anywhere from three to four minutes or more left in the game.

"The bench will communicate early with a goalie to let him know exactly when to be ready. Someone will let him know at a whistle when to be looking for his instructions and that the bench will be ready for him. So I think it's an analytics thing more than anything.

"I honestly think that if analytics weren't involved, most coaches would probably be more comfortable still pulling them around the 90-second mark."

COACHES CHALLENGE

Since the 2015–16 season, NHL head coaches have had the ability to use video replay to challenge goals that came as a result of offside plays and goaltender interference. Much of this stems from a playoff game in Montreal in 2015, when Nikita Kucherov scored an overtime goal that appeared to be offside, leading Tampa Bay to a win over Montreal.

Coaches have had a modicum of success with challenges over the years, with Pittsburgh's Mike Sullivan leading the league in 2021–22. Sullivan was a perfect 8–0, including six wins on offside challenges, tying him with Peter Laviolette for the top spot in that category. Laviolette led all coaches with 10 total challenges, finishing with a 7–3 record.

Sullivan leads all active coaches with a record of 34–26 on coach's challenges since going behind the Pittsburgh bench in December 2015. He's 19–8 when challenging goaltender interference situations and 15–18 on offside challenges.

Success on the challenges doesn't exactly ensure job safety though, as four of the top ten winningest coaches in 2021–22 were all fired at the end of the season: Bob Boughner (San Jose, 7–2), Bruce Cassidy (Boston, 5–2), Jeff Blashill (Detroit, 6–3) and Peter DeBoer (Vegas, 5–0).

Blashill actually has more wins (38) than Sullivan during this same time period, but he was fired by the Red Wings on April 30, 2022. During his seven seasons in Detroit, Blashill had 60 failures among his 98 total challenges, including 43 alone on goaltender interference.

Other notable challenge records among active head coaches include Jon Cooper (26–33), Peter Laviolette (28–22), Jared Bednar (25–20), Peter DeBoer (24–46), and John Tortorella (18–32).

VIDEO GAMES

There seem to be as many coaches on the bench as there are players some nights. And that's not accounting for the "eyes in the sky" that sit upstairs in the press box. They are the ones relaying information to the bench coaches through ear pieces. This information could be as simple as reminding a player about his positioning, or it could be alerting the bench to a possible replay challenge opportunity that looked more obvious from the press box view.

The players and coaches at ice level also have access to on-demand video available through iPads that are stored on the bench, using an application known as iBench.

The iBench product made its NHL debut during the 2017 Stanley Cup playoffs and immediately found success with Pittsburgh, the eventual Stanley Cup champions that year. The program was created by XOS Digital, a subsidiary of Catapult Sports, the same company that specializes in the wearable training devices.

At its simplest form, iBench is essentially a DVR for the game. Users can fast forward and rewind the video feed as it's coming in. The advantage of the application is that the team's video coach in the locker room can tag the key events that occur throughout the period, and have those appear on the iPad as well.

Players on the bench are able to go in and view those key events using the iPads. Depending on the situation in the game, a player could pull up all his faceoffs that night, or even just look back at his previous shift to figure out why a golden scoring opportunity went awry.

IBench serves a purpose for both coaches and players, but it's all up to the coaching staff of each team as to how they execute the product.

"There's a couple of different use cases in terms of how teams will leverage iBench during the course of play. One example is where a player is bringing something that they're seeing on the on the video to the attention of the coach. Maybe they're making that adjustment on the bench, or maybe it's ultimately something they're going to talk about in the locker room during the intermission," explains Bill McCarthy of Catapult Sports.

"The second piece of it is that both the coach and the player have the ability to flag or create their own event, even while they're on the bench during the game. That event then goes back to their video coach in the locker room. So for example, a coach can flag a key event that's occurred in the period. And then during intermission, go back and review that. It's just another point of reference for their in-game decision-making."

All thirty-two teams are using the in-game product, with another twenty-six actively using the compatible Thunder video system used by coaches for pre-scouting the opposition and additional video breakdowns.

Each team is allowed a league-mandated three iPads on the bench. (These are separate from the video monitors that are placed under the bench for the coaches.) All thirty-two arenas in the league have been configured with a dedicated Wi-Fi network, and the league assigns staff to manage all the infrastructure to ensure that that environment is configured correctly. Probably not a bad idea considering how glitchy and unpredictable some arena Wi-Fi networks can be for the fans.

Taking into consideration that Catapult's wearable data is tracked by numerous teams around the league, McCarthy sees a time where that confluence of information will also be available during games and incorporated into the program.

"I think a lot of that will be driven through our ability to integrate additional data points. Today, we have coaching points coming in. Eventually, we want to be able to begin integrating our wearable information to go along with the live data. There's probably a crossroads between data and video that will, again, help the coaches really make those decisions during a game."

NOT A FAN?

The iBench program definitely serves a very useful purpose during games, but it has its detractors. By now you've probably all seen the video that went viral during the 2022 Stanley Cup playoffs. Frustrated by the sight of his teammate Mika Zibanejad watching video of a missed breakaway during Game 6 of their first-round series against Pittsburgh, Chris Kreider grabbed the iPad from Zibanejad and tossed it away.

To no surprise, there have also been some strong opinions within the coaching fraternity.

When asked by reporters in April 2022 about how technology has continued to grow within the game in recent years, New Jersey head coach Lindy Ruff didn't mince any words.

"I think the iPads sometimes are a distraction. Players are grabbing for iPads constantly. There's times I'd just like to take the iPads and throw them away. I sense that almost everybody's looking at them.

"Sometimes when there's a mistake, they're looking at justification, that it might not be me. If you're barking out something we weren't good enough at, automatically somebody's reaching back and grabbing it and they want to go, 'Come on, that wasn't me.'"

CLOSING THOUGHTS

So, Dave Barr, what do you think about iBench and the use of video during games?

"I think every coach is different in regards to whether they like it on the bench or not. I personally think it's a distraction. What are players normally doing? They're watching their last shift and wondering *How did the other team get the puck there? I don't understand.* So they're probably sitting with a linemate staring at the iPad and now they're missing what's going on during the play. To me that is almost a distraction from staying engaged in the game—seeing what the other team is doing, seeing what we're doing. In my eyes I think it can wait until intermission.

"If a player asks me to show him a clip during intermission, I'd say no problem at all. We can call the video coach and ask him to grab that last scoring chance against us and have it ready for me. As soon as we walk in the dressing room it will be ready to go so we'd grab our computers and go talk to the player. To me, that's a much better teaching environment, as opposed to being on the bench with so much going on around you that is probably more important.

"I tend to agree with Lindy in that regard. But I think there is some benefit during things that require immediate attention like the power play or PK. If I notice that a team is using their third breakout and we didn't [have] a chance to talk about it earlier because I didn't think they were going to use it, I can get out the iPad and show that video right away.

"I think it's relevant for a few things and helpful for a few things. But for the most part, I think it's better for the entire bench if players aren't constantly staring at video during the game. It's like sitting at a table with a bunch of friends and everybody's looking at their phones. It's the same idea in my eyes.

"It's not the worst thing to do it when you think it's needed. But it's not like there aren't other TVs on the bench because there are other monitors right where the coaches are standing. The player can always turn around and look at that if they want. If we want to see a replay of a scoring chance, we can always ask the video coach to pull up that clip and then it's on the monitors right by our feet. So that's something that we can do that helps us control how they're getting feedback on the bench."

8

THE NHL DRAFT

When Colorado was dealt lemons, they went out and made the best damn lemonade they possibly could.

The Avs finished dead last in the NHL in 2016–17, posting an abysmal record of 22–56–4. Their 48 total points were 21 fewer than twenty-ninth place Vancouver, and they allowed 112 more goals (278) than they scored (166). All told, they put together one of the worst NHL seasons in more than a decade.

Their reward for being so inept was having the best odds in the draft lottery. At 18 percent, Colorado had by far the best chance of being awarded the number-one pick in the 2017 Entry Draft.

Not so fast.

Just like the regular season, things didn't exactly go Colorado's way on lottery night. Not only did they not get the number-one pick, they dropped all the way down to fourth behind New Jersey, Philadelphia, and Dallas—teams that finished twenty-seventh, nineteenth, and twenty-fourth respectively. It was also the fifth time in the previous six seasons where the team that finished last didn't win the lottery.

But if hindsight is a thing, Colorado absolutely won the lottery that year.

After the Devils surprised a few draft pundits by grabbing Swiss-born forward Nico Hischier with the first pick, Philadelphia selected highly-touted prospect Nolan Patrick second overall, followed by the Stars taking Finnish defenseman Miro Heiskanen in the third spot.

With the fourth overall selection, Colorado opened some eyes by taking babyfaced defenseman Cale Makar from the Brooks

Bandits of the Alberta Junior Hockey League. Hardly a household name at the time, Makar had been projected to be taken anywhere from fifth overall to thirteenth.

It's been a whirlwind for Makar ever since. Three days after winning the 2019 Hobey Baker Award as the top US college hockey player, Makar made his NHL debut during the 2019 Stanley Cup playoffs and scored the game-winning goal in his first game.

Makar then took home the Calder Trophy in 2020 as the league's top rookie, won the Norris Trophy as the NHL's best defenseman in 2022, and less than a week later, was awarded the 2022 Conn Smythe Trophy as the MVP of the playoffs, leading Colorado to their second Stanley Cup title.

Makar joined some elite company by winning both the Conn Smythe Trophy and Norris Trophy in the same year. The only two other defensemen to do it? Bobby Orr (1970, 1972) and Nicklas Lidström (2002).

If there was a redraft of the 2017 NHL Draft, there's no doubt Makar, the player some analysts thought might last until the middle of the first round, would be the consensus number-one pick.

Welcome to the unpredictable nature of the NHL draft.

Of all the data and science involved in every sport, perhaps the most inexact science of them all is the annual draft process. Teams employ countless resources and spend an abundance of time scouring the globe to stockpile their cupboards with prospect capital for years to come.

In the NHL, that means trying to figure out the mind and body of a teenager who is likely still in high school and his best years may be five years down the road. Such is the science of the NHL Entry Draft, where highly-paid hockey executives take their best shot at drafting an 18-year-old kid to potentially become the face of a professional sports franchise.

AGE ISN'T JUST A NUMBER

At the crux of any discussion about the NHL draft is the age limit.

There are three groups of players eligible to be selected in the annual NHL Entry Draft: a player who turns 18 on or before September 15 in the year of that draft; players that don't turn 20 prior to December 31 of the draft year; and non-North American players can be drafted at any age as long as they turn 18 before September 15.

It's almost unfathomable to think of the pressure these kids are under at such a young age. Looking back at the 18-year-old version of me, I was going into my senior year of high school and still had no clue what I wanted to be when I would (eventually) grow up.

Granted, the future for these kids has been predetermined for many years prior. In most cases they've been living away from home while playing junior hockey or attending college. European players are forced to play in men's leagues as teenagers, or move to North America to play junior hockey.

The spotlight often finds them earlier as well. Sidney Crosby and Connor McDavid had already made appearances on *Hockey Night in Canada* as teenagers. Starring roles in international under-18 and under-20 tournaments also made household names out of such future stars as Eric Lindros, John Tavares, Leon Draisaitl, and Trevor Zegras.

"There are so many things at play when it comes to evaluating players for the draft. But because of the variables surrounding how different we are as people, I think that age is the greatest variable of all when it comes to this process," explains Sam Cosentino, junior hockey and draft analyst for Sportsnet in Canada. "Not only are we trying to predict what kind of hockey player someone is going to become, it's also about looking at a 17-year-old and trying to figure out what kind of person they're going to be. That's a pretty difficult thing because they just haven't lived enough life yet."

Hockey's rush to judgment is definitely unlike the other major sports.

In a deep dive by the data-driven website fivethirtyeight.com, the average age of a first-round pick in the NFL was 21.7 years old in 2018, which was actually down from 22.6 in 2000. Since the NFL draft requires players to be three years removed from high school, players will normally be at least 20 on draft night.

The youngest player in the 2022 NFL Draft was running back Isaiah Spiller, who was 20 years old when he was selected in the fourth round by the Los Angeles Chargers.

Eight of the top ten picks in the 2022 NFL Draft were 21 years old. The other two were 20, including wide receiver Drake London, who was the second-youngest player selected in the draft when he was taken eighth overall by Atlanta.

Let's compare this to the 2022 NHL Draft, where each of the top ten selections were all 18 years old when they were taken, including the No. 1 overall pick Juraj Slafkovsky who was chosen by Montreal.

Adley Rutschman, the top prospect in Major League Baseball, was 21 years old when he was selected first overall by Baltimore in the 2019 MLB Draft. Rutschman didn't make his MLB debut for the Orioles until May 21, 2022—nearly three years after he was drafted.

Even superstar-in-waiting Bryce Harper had to bide his time. Harper was just 17 years old (he would turn 18 in October) when Washington made him the top selection in the 2010 MLB Draft. He didn't make his Nats debut until 2012, but Harper proved to be worth the wait. Harper was named the National League's Rookie of the Year in 2012, and has gone on to capture a pair of MVP awards.

ON THE FAST TRACK

Being selected No. 1 overall in the NHL is pretty much a guarantee of turning pro immediately. In a salary cap world, teams are more eager than ever before to get high-end young talent in the lineup sooner than later, while paying them entry-level salaries.

Some draft years offer up some no-brainers for the top spot, including studs like Patrick Kane (2007), Steven Stamkos (2008), Nathan MacKinnon (2013), Connor McDavid (2015), and Auston Matthews (2016). It made perfect sense to get these players to the NHL right away, and their stats ever since haven't proven otherwise.

Of course there are also the outliers. Say hello to 2012 first overall pick Nail Yakupov. The cries of "Fail for Nail" rang out all season as the league's bottom-feeders vied for the coveted forward, with Edmonton eventually getting their guy. This was the third year in a row Edmonton won the draft lottery, as Yakupov joined Taylor Hall (2010) and Ryan Nugent-Hopkins (2011) in some dubious company.

Yakupov showed flashes in his rookie campaign, playing in all 48 games of the lockout-shortened 2012–13 season. He scored what would turn out to be a career-high 17 goals, and his 31 points put him fourth in team scoring. Unfortunately it was all downhill from there.

The much-maligned Yakupov played three more seasons in Edmonton, including a career-best 33 points in 2014–15 to go along with a team-worst minus-35. After a pair of nondescript seasons with St. Louis and Colorado, Yakupov said *do svidaniya* to the NHL in 2018, and has been plying his trade in Russia's Kontinental Hockey League ever since.

As rare as it's been in recent years, not every top pick has made his NHL debut mere months after he's been drafted.

After being taken in the top spot in 2021, Owen Power became the first number one overall selection to not go directly to the NHL since Erik Johnson in 2006. It wasn't like Power couldn't have made the jump. The global pandemic played a role in Power's decision-making.

After a freshman season at the University of Michigan that was riddled with COVID restrictions, Power wanted to get the full college experience with his Wolverines teammates and take a shot at an NCAA title. Following a semifinal loss to Denver in the 2021 Frozen Four, Power signed his three-year entry level contract with the Sabres on April 8, 2022, and made his NHL debut four days later in Toronto.

JUST WAIT AND SEE

Despite their advance billing and elevated draft status, some prospects just take a little longer to spread their wings. They need a little more time to marinate, if you will. Edmonton's Leon Draisaitl is one of those players.

Draisaitl was chosen third overall in a top-heavy 2014 draft class that featured the top two picks Aaron Ekblad (Florida) and Sam Reinhart (Buffalo).

While Reinhart was a work-in-progress physically, Ekblad and Draisaitl were fully grown men in a teenager's body. Not only were they both imposing physical specimens, they seemed mature beyond their years when I spoke to them at a media gathering prior to the draft. It's no secret that these kids are taught at a young age how to conduct themselves with the media, but there was something easy and comfortable about how Draisaitl handled himself.

Draisaitl made the Oilers' opening-night lineup in 2014–15, but he struggled mightily in his rookie season. He only contributed one goal and two assists in his first 10 games, despite averaging about 13 minutes of ice time per game. He was sent back to junior hockey after 37 games, finishing with just two goals and nine points.

Despite being dubbed "maddeningly inconsistent" early in his career by an Edmonton writer, all Draisaitl has done since then is establish himself as one of the game's elite players. He's put up 100-point seasons in three of the past four years, has a pair of 50-goal seasons to his credit, and was named league MVP in 2019–20. I guess you could say the Oilers nailed this pick.

DRAFT PLANNING

No two drafts are ever alike, so it's impossible to map out a consistent strategy. There's always going to be high-end talent in the early part of the first round, but it's not always guaranteed that player will step in and immediately change the fate of a franchise. Some years there will be one of those no-brainers at the top, and other years could be a toss-up among the first five, ten, or even fifteen players.

Once you get past the first ten picks in the draft, there's not a ton of separation in talent. The same can also be said for the bottom half of the first round, and what you're likely going to see in rounds five and six.

Making sure you get it right early on can often make or break a franchise for years to come. Chris Gear, a former assistant general manager with Vancouver, explains why a swing and miss in the early rounds can be costly.

"The first two rounds are where you find your surest bets. Those are the guys that everybody's more confident about because they're more fully formed and they've dominated for a longer period of time. These guys aren't late bloomers. These are the picks you need to hit on.

"I'd say a third-rounder is a building block, but even that might be pushing it. From the third round down is a bit of a crapshoot. But if you do the work and you've got good scouts, you can find gems in every round."

Mining those gems can prove to be more valuable than hitting paydirt in the early rounds. Look no further than Tampa Bay as a team that has capitalized on their success in the later rounds.

On their way to back-to-back Stanley Cups in 2020 and 2021, the Lightning relied heavily on several players who inexplicably slid down the draft boards of every team in the league.

Brayden Point (third round, 2014) was second in team scoring during each of Tampa Bay's Cup runs, and his absence was sorely missed in their 2022 loss to Colorado.

Ondrej Palat (seventh round, 2011) leads the NHL in postseason even-strength goals (24) and game-winning goals (eight) since 2020.

You also can't forget about the valuable playoff and regular season contributions from the likes of forwards Anthony Cirelli (third round, 2015), Ross Colton (fourth round, 2016), and Alex Killorn (third round, 2007).

I'd even throw Nikita Kucherov (second round, 2011) into this conversation. Sure, he was a second-round pick. But it also means that fifty-seven other teams passed on a guy whose 93 points in 71 games led the entire NHL in playoff scoring from 2020 to 2022.

The Lightning have shown in recent years that giving the rose to the right person can be a marriage made in heaven.

"A team should be commended, applauded, and celebrated for their ability to do their work in that space, where few others have been able to," said Cosentino. "I look at it in two ways. Yeah, I would like to see a little bit more certainty. And I'd like to take some of the guesswork out of it, and allow those people to further develop both mentally and physically.

"But I also have a great amount of respect for the people who can do it and do it successfully continuously later in the draft like a Tampa Bay."

TOUGH CHOICES

One of the toughest decisions teams have to make each year, especially early in the draft, is whether to draft for organizational need or simply take the best player available on the board when it comes time to pick.

Because every team's draft board is different, there is no hard and fast rule with this. Just because a media draft guru like Bob McKenzie thinks Player X is the best available at that time, it may not fit with how a team may have mapped out their draft strategy. Filling holes on a depth chart may be more important to some teams than stockpiling the best players available.

"I always think best available is the right play because you don't know how it's going to evolve," says Gear. "You may be weak in a certain position now, but you have no guarantee when that guy will be ready. And positional needs can change in your organization over time based on things like trades and free agency."

Gear knows firsthand the perils of drafting for need over best available, and it happened very early for Vancouver in the 2016 draft.

"Did we always do that? No. In 2016 we drafted a kid named Olli Juolevi fifth overall because we felt like we were desperate to have a defenseman in the system. In doing so, we passed on Matthew Tkachuk, who was a forward, which we felt we knew we could use. I felt we could use a little bit of everything. But I think the organizational belief was that the need was more dire on defense. And so to take Juolevi over Tkachuk? That turned out to be a big mistake."

Calling it a mistake is being polite. Tkachuk went one pick later to Calgary at number six, and he is considered by many to be the second-best player from that draft class behind Auston Matthews. Tkachuk put up career highs in goals (42), assists (62), and points (104) in 2021–22 while playing on one of the league's top lines alongside Johnny Gaudreau and Elias Lindholm.

As for Juolevi? He only ended up played 23 career games for Vancouver, collecting two goals and an assist. He was dealt to Florida in October 2021, and would finish the season on his third team in less than a year after being claimed off waivers in March 2022 as somewhat of a reclamation project by Detroit.

THE COMBINE

The top draft-eligible players make their way to Buffalo each spring to be poked and prodded—both physically and mentally—by the teams courting them for future employment. As one person likes to describe it to me, the combine is gym class with job interviews.

A total of ninety-six prospects were invited to attend the 2022 NHL Scouting Combine that took place in Buffalo for six days in late May and early June. The ninety-six players were all listed in NHL Central Scouting's final rankings of North American and International skaters (sixty-three forwards and thirty defensemen) and three goalies, essentially making up the group of players expected to be taken in the first three rounds of the 2022 draft.

A staple of the draft process since 1994, the combine has been based at KeyBank Center and the adjacent Harborcenter rink complex in Buffalo since 2015. (The 2020 and 2021 combines were both cancelled due to the pandemic.) Fitness testing is administered on the floor of the Harborcenter main rink, with player interviews taking place in various locations.

Prior to moving to Buffalo in 2015, the fitness testing took place at a convention center near the Toronto airport, with the interviews scheduled at the surrounding hotels.

While it's nowhere near the media circus that the annual NFL combine has become, the NHL version has definitely grown in prominence since flying under the radar during its early years.

PLAYER INTERVIEWS

With the key decision-makers (general managers and scouts) from all thirty-two teams gathered in one location for the week, the prospects get one last chance to make a final impression on the people that have been evaluating their on-ice performance over the last few years. The majority of in-person interviews take place from Monday through Friday inside the suites at KeyBank Center, along with a Marriott hotel that is also part of the complex.

Teams request interviews with any players they are interested in drafting. Even if a team knows they likely won't have a chance at drafting a particular player because of their draft position, this also offers them the opportunity to evaluate a player for possible transaction in the future.

For many teams, this could be the first time they've been able to sit down and talk in-depth with a prospect. They already know what the player's physical attributes are, and these gatherings are intended to offer a more personal look at the player.

There's a lot to be said about the exercise and sports science that goes on throughout the draft process. Being physically able to compete is one thing. But getting inside the head of a prospect to learn the mental and emotional side is another animal altogether. General managers and coaches always talk about building a winning culture, and that culture can take roots in these interviews.

Questions can run the gamut from hockey to personal, to putting a player in a hypothetical scenario to see what kind of response they give. One of the more popular approaches is to ask a player if they value an individual achievement over a team accomplishment.

There are also a few curveballs that get tossed. At the 2022 combine, Shane Wright, who ended up being selected fourth overall by Seattle, told reporters he was asked what twenty-five multiplied by twenty-five was. (The answer is 625 for those playing at home.) Another player was asked if he had downloaded one of the new online betting apps on his phone. It's all about learning what really makes a player tick to get a better idea of their character and personality.

Gear said the Canucks always had a solid list of questions prepared for each prospect, but it wasn't uncommon for them to go off-script during the interview if a prospect's answers took them in a different direction.

In later years, the Canucks also enlisted their sports psychologist when doing prep work for the interviews. When COVID forced the interviews into a Zoom call situation for 2020 and 2021, Gear explains how that sports psychologist came in handy on a different level.

"Because it was a COVID situation we had the sports psychologist actually sitting on those Zoom calls with us. Normally, he wouldn't have accompanied us to the combine. And it was neat, because he was trained to pick up on visual cues that we weren't.

"It was little things like where did the player look when he was asked a question—did they make eye contact, or are they always looking down? He had analysis on simple things like that. And sometimes his assessment of a player was very different than the scout's because he comes from a completely different place."

The attitude of a prospect entering the interview room can have a significant bearing on the outcome. If a player is surrounded by family and friends telling him that he's a surefire top-ten pick, then it might not sit well with him when a team picking in the eighteenth position requests an interview with him.

Rather than looking at it as being the opportunity of a lifetime to just get drafted into the NHL, some guys are more concerned with their image and status. According to Gear, teams pick up on that quickly and it doesn't usually end well.

"We had some guys that just didn't want to be in that room with us, and it was obvious. There were other guys that were just kind of nonverbal or looked down a lot and just seemed like they didn't care. You have to take that with a grain of salt because there are guys that are introverts and extroverts, and you don't want to base too much of an opinion on that.

"But there were some guys whose answers are either not very well thought out, or they're a little snarky. You definitely get a different impression from some guys. You can usually tell pretty quickly if that guy will be a good fit in your dressing room, or if he has the maturity that you're looking for."

LET'S GET PHYSICAL

The players are put through a series of fitness tests during the week in front of a captive audience of team personnel and strength coaches to test their overall power, speed, and endurance. Medical examinations are administered to each prospect, and a player must be cleared by a doctor to take part in the fitness testing that follows.

Seven of the most notable tests take place on the combine's final day: standing height, wingspan, standing long jump, bench press, pro agility test, pull-ups, and the always grueling (and somewhat entertaining, depending on your perspective) Wingate cycle ergonometer test.

What is the Wingate? Say hello to the black cloud that hangs over the fitness testing for the entire week. Players fear this more than taking a slap shot in the groin. They've lost sleep worrying about this test, and their lunch while being tested on it.

Designed to measure power and level of fatigue, a player rides the bike for forty-five seconds, using ten-second intervals of all-out pedaling. This is actually a change from years ago when a player had to go all-out for thirty seconds while the tension increased.

None of these tests are a pass or fail situation. For the most part, they are really just a snapshot in time of where a player is in his development path. However, a player that puts up some impressive testing numbers in a few of the stations can definitely open a few more eyes.

If anything, scoring poorly on any of the fitness testing is just another example of an 18-year-old not being as physically mature as they could be in the next two to three years. It often shows how the player needs to improve his workout and conditioning program, and focus on certain areas of required growth.

Maybe, like being able to do a pull-up. Sam Bennett knows all about this.

Projected as one of the top prospects in the 2014 draft, Bennett blew up social media at the combine that year when he was unable to do a single pull-up in testing.

As a comparison, Northeastern University forward Jack Hughes (taken in the second round by Los Angeles) led all prospects when he successfully completed nineteen consecutive pull-ups at the 2022 combine.

Bennett, whose draft profile listed him as being just over six feet tall and 178 pounds, was coming off a 2013–14 season where he collected 36 goals and 91 points in 57 games for the OHL's Kingston Frontenacs as a 17-year-old. At points in the season, he was considered by some to be the top prospect available.

Bennett, who ended up being drafted fourth overall by Calgary, shrugged off all the attention at the time. Like many in the media, Ken Campbell of *The Hockey News* didn't put too much stock in Bennett's combine blunder.

"So the fact that Sam Bennett could not complete one chin-up at the NHL scouting combine recently is an interesting, and amusing, story, but all it means is that he's clueless. Like a lot of the kids in the draft, Bennett probably believed until now that he was working really, really hard off the ice. And while it might create a red flag for some teams, anyone passing on him because he can't do a chin-up—actually he reported on Monday that he can now do two—risks ignoring the player who might turn out to be the best of the 2014 draft."

Bennett has yet to live up to Campbell's hype, but he did record career-highs in goals (28) and points (49) with the Florida Panthers in 2021–22. Now 26 years old, Bennett has also filled out to 6-foot-1 and 195 pounds.

That same combine ignominy also befell Casey Mittelstadt before he was taken eighth overall by Buffalo in 2017.

Not only was Mittelstadt unable to do a pull-up, he completed just one rep on his bench press test. Listed as being 6-foot-1 and (a doughy) 201 pounds at the time, Mittelstadt now checks in at 6-foot-1 and 196 pounds. Injuries have slowed Mittelstadt's development, but he's shown flashes of why he was selected so high, and is quietly emerging as a key piece of Buffalo's young core of talent.

Not being able to do a pull-up isn't the end of the world, and as we've seen, it's definitely not going to curtail anyone's NHL dreams. Other than being social media fodder for a few hours, a poor score on a particular test is just another way for a team to go about their evaluation player process.

"You do have to consider the testing results a little bit. But it's got to be in context, too. Some guys are just smaller and weaker, but they can still play. It's a balancing act," says Gear.

"It also makes you wonder if he's training hard enough? Is he putting the work in? And do they have a strong enough commitment that they can continue to improve as they get older? As they grow, if they don't put the work in, other people are gonna pass them by. These are all the things we look at with the testing."

THE GOALIE MARKET

Considering the importance of the position, one of the constant quirks of the entry draft is how few goalies are selected in the first and second rounds each year.

Since 2000, only two goalies have been selected first overall: Rick DiPietro in 2000 by the New York Islanders and Marc-Andre Fleury by Pittsburgh in 2003.

In the twelve drafts from 2011 to 2022, only thirty-seven goalies were selected in the first two rounds. Eight were taken in the first round, with the remaining twenty-nine coming in round two. With a total of 740 players drafted in the first two rounds during those years, this means that just 5 percent of those were goalies.

Of the thirty-seven goalies, twenty-three of them have gone on to play in the NHL. Notable names from this group include Andrei Vasilevskiy (2012, first round), Thatcher Demko (2014, second round), Ilya Samsonov (2015, first round), and Carter Hart (2016, second round).

If you're curious, 2022 Vezina Trophy winner Igor Shesterkin was the fourteenth goalie selected in the 2014 draft when he was picked by the New York Rangers in the fourth round. The highest drafted goalie in 2014? Mason McDonald was taken thirty-fourth overall by the Calgary Flames. McDonald has yet to see any NHL action.

There are a few theories floating around to try and explain why exactly this has become such a regular occurrence. The main train of thought is that goalies typically don't get as much playing time in their draft-eligible season, so it's difficult to project their development track.

Because it's rare for a 17- or 18-year-old goalie to be a team's main starter—especially at the major junior level—scouts don't really have the stats or viewings to see how they perform at that level and how they will project down the road.

"Very rarely does a guy go in as a 16-year-old and play. So you've essentially missed out on your 16-year-old season because you're just you're playing backup to an older guy on a team that wants to win," explains Cosentino. "Then as a 17-year-old he'll probably play some more in his draft year, and some of the high-end guys may even become starters.

"Now all of a sudden as a GM you're in a position to draft a guy and predict his future when you may have only seen him in a limited viewing of 40 to 45 games. I don't know how you can be expected to make a long-term determination on what that guy is going to be when essentially he's played 40 games."

Even without an extensive playing resume to review, some teams will often add another layer to the evaluation process. That was the case with Vancouver when they drafted Demko thirty-sixth overall in 2014.

Coming off a successful run with the United States National Development Team, Demko went to Boston College in his draft year and quickly established himself as the team's top goalie, posting an impressive 16–5–3 record in his freshman season. Despite those numbers, that still meant the Canucks were only working with 24 games to project Demko's future. That left the Canucks brass with a little more homework to do.

"Every year we'd have our goalie coach, Ian Clark, do a deeper evaluation on goaltending prospects based on just their physical attributes, starting with the basics like size, height and weight, and quickness," said Gear. "Then he would analyze their game in terms of whether he thought they could grow into something. He wouldn't even care what their stats were. He'd watch little things like speed, recovery time, and how fast a guy can get in and out of the butterfly position.

"From there Ian would provide his recommendations on who we should draft based on observing the player, regardless of his team's record or his personal stats. If that player had the physical tools that Ian identified, we probably took a longer look at him. That was the case with Demko."

Another theory that has been discussed is that a general manger doesn't want to take the chance on somebody who could still be four years away from making the roster. Because the shelf life of some general managers is typically three to five years, they prefer to select a player who can have an immediate impact while they are trying to contend, not years down the road.

I decided to put this theory to the test using the using the first two rounds of the five drafts from 2017 to 2021. Listed below are the names of each goalie, the team that selected them, with the name of the general manager at the time in brackets. An X is listed with any general manager no longer with that team.

2021	Sebastian Cossa, Detroit (Steve Yzerman); Jesper Wallstedt, Minnesota (Bill Guerin)
2020	Yaroslav Askarov, Nashville (David Poile); Drew Commesso, Chicago (Stan Bowman - X); Joel Blomqvist, Pittsburgh (Jim Rutherford - X)
2019	Spencer Knight, Florida (Dale Tallon - X); Pyotr Kochetkov, Carolina (Don Waddell); Mads Sogaard, Ottawa (Pierre Dorion); Hunter Jones, Minnesota (Paul Fenton - X)
2018	Olof Lindbom, New York Rangers (Jeff Gorton - X); Olivier Rodrigue, Edmonton (Peter Chiarelli - X)
2017	Jake Oettinger, Dallas (Jim Nill); Ukko-Pekka Luukkonen, Buffalo (Jason Botterill - X)

Of the thirteen general managers listed, seven of them are no longer with that team. It is notable that five of the seven were from the earlier 2017 to 2019 window, adding credence to the shelf life of a general manager.

(It should also be noted that Rutherford resigned from Pittsburgh in 2021 for personal reasons, and Bowman resigned from the Blackhawks amid the team's sexual abuse scandal in 2021.)

While Gear didn't summarily dismiss this theory, he said there are typically a couple of other factors that need to be considered when drafting a goalie in the first two rounds.

"You need to consider where a team is at in their development lifecycle. If you're a GM that has a really good team, and maybe even an AHL team that has lots of depth, you can take a chance on taking a goalie higher because your team is going to be set for a few years and you can wait for that goalie to develop.

"Or, if you've got a starter who's getting up in years, and maybe a backup who's getting older, then you might as well try to get one that's highly sought after or highly ranked. I think it's more about where your team is at and how the goaltending situation is shaping up over the next few years."

9

CONTACT & INJURIES

Numbers play a big part in all sports, and the game of hockey is no different. But not all the numbers pertain to events that happen on the ice. Injuries are a significant part of sports, and being able to quantify their impact has become very important.

Let me introduce you to my old friend, man games lost.

Though it's not an official league stat, a man game lost refers to any game missed by a rostered player who is unable to play due to injury. Any player that doesn't play due to suspension or personal reasons doesn't count, along with healthy scratches. If a player is recalled from the minors and is injured during their time with the big club, any game missed is counted as a man game lost, as an injured player cannot be returned to the minors until completely healthy.

Here's the catch: man games lost are tracked manually by each team. I know, because I used to do it for Buffalo. Keeping a running tabulation of man games lost and individual injury reports was a staple of my game notes every night. Each injured player was listed with their injury designation assigned by the team and how many games they had missed.

The website NHL Injury Viz has taken this reporting to an entirely new level. Using the injury information reported by the media (via the game notes), NHL Injury Viz aggregates that info into a collection of various charts and graphs to visually display the impact of injuries. They also keep a yearly listing of all player injuries and their man games lost.

Using this information, I decided to take a look back at the man games lost totals from the last five full seasons from 2014–15 to

2018–19. (The 2019–20 and 2020–21 seasons were both left out of this exercise because of their abbreviated scheduling.)

And despite 2021–22 being the league's first full 82-game slate in three years, this season wasn't included due to the COVID-related illnesses and restrictions that remained in place since the league shutdown because of the pandemic in March 2020.

Montreal (599), Arizona (597), Vegas (505), and Philadelphia (502) each surpassed the 500-game plateau in 2021–22, with four others cracking 400. In the five seasons that were tracked, it was a rarity for any team to exceed 300 man games lost in one season.

Thanks to the good folks at NHL Injury Viz, let's take a look at the top five teams with the most and fewest man games lost during the five-year period from 2014–15 to 2018–19.

Most:

Vancouver (1,696), Anaheim (1,540), Buffalo (1,483), New Jersey (1,421), and Colorado (1,392)

Vancouver consistently ranked among the most injured teams in each of these five seasons, including 459 man games lost in 2016–17, trailing only Colorado (487, 2014–15) and Columbus (507, 2014–15) for the single-season highs during this stretch.

Who wasn't in the lineup for Vancouver during these seasons was almost as notable as the players on the ice. Impact players including Alex Edler, Bo Horvat, Jacob Markstrom, and Chris Tanev all missed significant amounts of time for the Canucks. Vancouver played below .500 hockey in four of the five seasons and only qualified for the playoffs once.

Looking to put this injury nightmare behind them, it should come as no surprise the Canucks fired their head athletic therapist and head strength and conditioning coach following the 2021–22 season.

Fewest:

Washington (637), Chicago (762), Carolina (766), New York Rangers (789), and Minnesota (864).

Washington recorded the lowest season total of 49 man games lost in 2016–17 when they finished first in the Metropolitan Division with a record of 55–19–8. Not to be outdone, they also own the third lowest mark with just 87 man games lost during their Stanley Cup championship season in 2017–18. During these five seasons, only six teams had double-digit man games lost in one season, with Washington posting two of them.

The four other teams in this group also achieved significant success during this stretch, highlighted by Chicago's Stanley Cup title in 2014–15. Carolina and the New York Rangers both played in the Eastern Conference finals, and Minnesota made four playoff appearances in five seasons.

Teams have been able to qualify for the playoffs with an unusually high number of man games lost, but it definitely doesn't happen very often.

In eighteen postseasons from 2003–04 to 2021–22, the data tracked by NHL Injury Viz says that just eight teams have made the playoffs when they've had more than 400 man games lost in a season. The St. Louis Blues lead the pack with 465 in 2008–09, and Los Angeles was the most recent to accomplish this with 414 in 2021–22. Four of the eight teams were eliminated in the first round, and the other four were bounced in round two.

INJURY TYPE

From your head to your toes and everywhere in between, no body part is spared from possible injury thanks to the speed and force involved in the game of hockey.

NHL Injury Viz compiled the data of all reported injuries in the 21 seasons from 2000 to 2022. In all there were 19,364 separate injuries ranging from a skin infection to a concussion. From these injuries, nearly 149,000 man games were lost over those 21 seasons. On average, each team has to deal with about 28 to 33 injuries each season.

Leading the way in this macabre marathon were knee and leg injuries, accounting for 17 percent of all man games lost. There were 2,119 instances, totaling 24,671 games. This should come as no surprise because of the typical severity of a knee injury. Anything involving an anterior cruciate ligament (ACL) or medial collateral ligament (MCL) typically involves surgery followed by an extensive rehab.

There were thirty-seven instances leaguewide of leg and knee injuries in 2021–22, resulting in 922 man games lost. Of these thirty-seven, fourteen players missed 20 or more, while another ten players missed between 10 and 20 games.

Checking in at the number two spot on the list with 10 percent of man games lost (15,540) is the always popular "lower body" injury. In fact, the 2,496 reported instances of a lower body injury over the last 21 seasons is the most of any category.

While we're on the topic, the "upper body" injury designation was reported 2,411 times, making up 9 percent (13,946) of the man games lost. The unforgettable "undisclosed/mid-body/soreness" designation appeared 1,079 times, amounting for 3 percent (3,841) of man games lost.

The simple fact that three of the vaguest injury descriptions combine for nearly 23 percent of the man games lost over the last 21 seasons is ridiculous. After all, upper body, mid-body, and lower body aren't official terminology. It's just another way for teams to play fast and loose with injury reporting, amid concerns of having an injured player targeted by the opposition upon return or as he tries to play through it.

If you think this injury chicanery is going to get any clearer, guess again. There appears to be a leaguewide buy-in and the train has already left the station. In 2021–22, the instances of upper body, lower body, and mid-body/soreness combined for 41 percent of all reported injuries.

There's no real definition as to what constitutes an upper or lower body injury; it's basically become an easy way for a coach to get out of providing actual information. Upper body could refer to anything between the groin and the head, while lower could range from a groin pull to a high ankle sprain.

This lack of injury transparency could also become an issue going forward as the NHL hitches its wagon to legalized sports gambling. Both the NFL and NBA have fairly rigid rules regarding injury reporting, while the NHL continues to look the other way.

Calgary coach Darryl Sutter vented about injury reporting to the media when he was asked about his team's health status before their second-round playoff series against Edmonton in 2022.

"Don't ask about injuries or who's playing anymore . . . The league should have a policy on it because, during the regular season, you're day-to-day, you're on IR for work, or you're LTIR, which is long-term. So why would that open up during the playoffs? Nobody should have to answer questions. Nobody should have to say it. Why should a coach come up and talk about someone who's injured? It's like, it's not right. That's like saying, 'Here's another cookie.'"

One of the players that Sutter was being asked about was defenseman Chris Tanev, who was injured in Game 6 of Calgary's first-round series against Dallas. Tanev was only able to play in the final two games of Calgary's five-game series loss to Edmonton, and it was later revealed that he was basically being held together with duct tape.

Two days after the series ended, it was announced that the 32-year-old Tanev would be undergoing surgery to repair a dislocated shoulder and torn labrum. There were also reports he'd been dealing with a sprained neck. Remarkably, Tanev and his bad wing averaged 21 minutes of ice time in the two games against Edmonton and was a plus-three.

Ironically, Calgary was the NHL's healthiest team in 2021–22 with a league-low 75 man games lost to injury. They were the only team to finish below 100, with Nashville's 147 being the next lowest total.

The Flames only reported thirteen separate injuries, with three players—Nick Ritchie (22), Tyler Pitlick (18), and Sean Monahan (15)—accounting for 55 of the 75 man games lost.

WALKING WOUNDED

Four other groups of injuries combined for 36 percent of man games lost over the 21 seasons, with each one checking in at 9 percent of the overall total.

There were 1,305 achilles/ankle/foot/toe injuries that resulted in 12,720 man games lost. The grouping of arm/hand/wrist was responsible for 13,405 man games lost through 1,298 separate instances.

To no surprise, concussions also appear very high on the list. Grouped with head and headaches, players missed a total of 13,517 games in 1,243 instances. Rounding out the group of four are the 1,105 collarbone/shoulder injuries that translated to 13,190 man games lost.

Two other groups of injuries were also notable but for different reasons.

There were 1,226 groin injuries (8,104 MGL) and 452 hip/pelvis/pubic injuries (4,470 MGL). The two combined to account for just 9 percent of the man games lost among all players, but they had a significant impact on goaltenders.

Groin injuries were responsible for 15 percent of all man games lost by goaltenders, while only having a minor impact on forwards (5 percent) and defensemen (4 percent). In addition, hip/pelvis/pubic injuries affected goalies (6 percent) more than forwards (3 percent) and blueliners (2 percent). Knee injuries were the leading cause of injury among goaltenders at 21 percent.

It should come as no surprise to see how goalies have become so prone to hip and groin injuries. As the position continues to evolve, the emphasis on mechanical and rotational movements take a toll on goaltenders through constant repetition of these movements in games and practices.

THE RISK REWARD

As goalies continue to deal with these injuries, sports science is trying to come up with ways to make them more preventable.

One of the global leaders in this field is Catapult, an Australian-based company that first came to prominence working with Australian rules football and European soccer teams, and their wearable technologies are now being used by 3,200 teams around the world.

Wearables have become an invaluable tool in the training world, and Catapult is considered by many to be the gold standard in this realm. Catapult has been in the hockey community for more than fifteen years focusing primarily on skaters, but they recently developed a program for goaltenders to help understand the unique physical demands of the position.

The Hockey Goalie Analytics solution was launched by Catapult in November 2021, using insights from six NHL teams to help uncover a 360-degree view of the movements and physical patterns of a goaltender. The goal is to increase performance and prevent the overloading that ultimately causes injuries.

Among the numerous metrics tracked by Catapult's analytics software are:

Down Count: The number of times a goalie shifts from feet to knees in a blocking position.

Goalie Load: The volume the goalie has experienced over a single session.

Goalie Load per Minute: The Goalie Load over a session duration, which provides a relative level of intensity for the athlete.

Asymmetry: The volume and intensity for both left and right directional movements on the ice.

Collecting the information is done using a 3.5-ounce device about the size of an AirPod case that is worn underneath the shoulder pads in a pouch or compression shirt. Through a series of algorithms originally formulated by Ben Peterson, who was Catapult's sports performance manager at that time, the device is able to track a variety of player movements from speed of stride to weight distribution while skating.

"Our data science team painstakingly looked at video, and then looked at the accelerometry data. There were about twenty-two key variables that indicated what the skating stride was. And then inside of that unit, there's also a gyroscope," says Patrick Love, customer success specialist with Catapult's hockey division. "So if the unit turns to the left, you can assume that you're pushing with your right side, same thing would be on the opposite end of the spectrum. That's essentially how it works with the accelerometer and the gyroscope."

(While it's not exactly an apples to apples comparison, the device works much like how an iPhone uses accelerometer data to collect up and down movements while walking for its Steps feature in the Health app.)

The goalie project was spearheaded by Adam Douglas, who is now the director of sport science and performance with Montreal. Douglas built on what Peterson had developed with the stride analysis, gearing it towards the movement of goaltenders. Love says the goal is to identify certain movement patterns that can cause injury over time.

"The biggest contributor to goalie load is when they go down. And one of the interesting things we've been seeing is the number of times when a goalie goes down like game, versus how many times we go down in a practice is vastly different.

"Let's say they go down in a game maybe thirty times. Whereas in a practice, you can see them go down about one hundred times or more. It's crazy how much more workload they're taking on in practice than in games. So rather than overworking them in practice, you kind of want the coaches to see that the maybe the game situation is not what's contributing to certain injury factors even or just physical wear and tear."

Collecting actual game data isn't an option for Catapult at the NHL level right now because the league doesn't allow the devices to be worn during games. Love describes this is a "suboptimal" situation, but they work with the users to figure out what the demands of the game are and then do a regression equation to get a decent estimate of what the game data would be.

Love says the options are almost limitless to what Catapult is able to measure for both skaters and goalies. But in terms of the most popular ways to analyze a player's performance, Love explains a few metrics that teams rely on more than others:

Volume metrics, in terms of how much work a player has done from a global volume standpoint. This would be the player load, which is just the changes in acceleration, forward and backwards, side to side, and up and down. And then locally, looking at the hips and groin with the skating load. This is the sum of the peak accelerations per stride, times the athlete's mass.

When it comes to intensity, there's some debate about what you would look for. You could do player load per minute, or skating load per minute. Another common one would be high-intensity work duration. This is the time spent in the highest threshold kind of similar to heart rate, the time spent in zone five.

Asymmetry can actually look at like the number of strides taken between the left and the right leg. And then also just the force produced on the left and the right leg.

To put it into context, someone who is considered an inefficient mover will likely have a higher workload, and efficient skaters typically have lower workloads. The inefficiency could be a result of the individual's skating stride, or an injury that is hampering fluidity of movement. In a game situation, this could cause a player to be out of position more, forcing them to work harder to recover. Having the right people in place to interpret this data is crucial to Catapult's effectiveness.

Each team will have a person dedicated to collecting the Catapult data and reviewing the results. Once a baseline set of numbers are established for a player, the Catapult specialist will be able to identify anything that looks unusual after a workout, something like stride length or ability to compete at a high level for their usual amount of time.

With injury mitigation being one of Catapult's main objectives, any red flags that go up will start conversations with the necessary individuals. In many ways, Catapult is no different of a diagnostic tool than the check engine light in your car.

"It's used in conjunction with a number of different things. If you see something that looks unusual, maybe it's time to have a conversation with your medical staff or strength coaches," says Love. "But then it's also looking at some of the other data that you're collecting from things like Force Plates, jump tests, and any other biomechanics evaluators. You definitely can get a fingerprint on a player, see where their baseline is, and if you're out of whack, at least start having that conversation."

So if Catapult is the check engine light, then maybe Rob Day is one of the mechanics that can fix the problem.

Day is the co-founder of Sports Science Solutions, a New Hampshire-based company that focuses on injury prevention and sports performance through cutting-edge video solutions.

An engineer by trade with an extensive coaching background, Day uses MotionIQ technology to assess an athlete's overall body fitness. Through the video analysis, they can identify any imbalances that might affect performance, along with reviewing body composition and muscle structure to ensure top performance levels and trying to avoid any potential injury concerns.

When it comes to hockey, Day focuses on two specific areas that will ultimately play an important role in performance success.

"The whole key to hockey is balance and stability. They have to be there first before you can get power and speed. We've seen a lot of power and speed without the without the balance and stability. That's like driving a Ferrari with bald tires in the rain."

The first step in the process is to assess an individual's overall body composition, similar to how it's done with the NHL and other professional sports leagues. This is a dryland-based situation where the athlete goes through a three-minute test that is recorded using a functional motor screen. Using a markerless system, the MotionIQ video analysis is able to detect more than 250,000 data points that can identify any issues with movement and mobility.

When possible, Day and his team can do an even deeper dive on a hockey player using sensors attached to the body. This allows them to extract additional body composition information while a player is skating on the ice.

Upon completion of the assessment, each athlete is provided with a comprehensive report detailing all the movement patterns that were studied, along with a list of any corrective training activities that can rectify certain issues.

"Using the movement patterns of an athlete, we can basically either predict an injury or try to prevent it from occurring. If a goalie is having issues with their hips, we can watch the video to see if it could be from how their feet are moving or if their knees are bending properly," explains Day. "We provide this information for them and they can use it [to] work with their trainer to help correct the movement patterns and hopefully avoid any kind of injury."

Day shared the example of an NCAA Division I goaltender they worked with a few years back. Using the MotionIQ video analysis, they detected an irregular movement in his knees that they thought could trigger potential hip issues down the road.

"When we pointed it out, he mentioned that he'd had his knee operated on three years ago. That made perfect sense, because the body will often adapt to any type of trauma and sometimes new movement patterns get developed out of that," Day said. "We explained that if he didn't correct it sooner than later, a hip injury was inevitable. So we walked him through everything, and made suggestions to his trainer on what areas to target. After the trainer worked to strengthen the muscles in his knees and hips, he came back six weeks later and tested without any issues. And he finished up his college career injury-free."

The ability to detect and even prevent injuries continues to evolve, but it's not going to advance unless athletes buy in to the science. I've seen firsthand at the NHL level where players were resistant to accepting advancements in science, especially as it pertained to their bodies. Just like analytics, players are often reluctant to look past anything beyond their personal stats.

With so many of today's athletes coming from the Gen Z demographic, technology is just a way of life for them. Not only do they embrace the data, they want to consume as much as possible, especially if it makes them better at what they do.

When it comes to Catapult, Love readily admits there's been an obvious shift in the mindset of how players view the science.

"I can definitely tell you this has changed over the last five years. When I started working in pro hockey, if I would have tried to tell some of the old-school guys 'Hey, we're going to put an accelerometer, a gyroscope, and a magnetometer on your back,' they would've looked at me like I was insane.

"Now, everybody's just kind of used to having data being collected on them, and then understanding what the data means. Guys want to know what their workload is at, because if they can't perform, then that's going to affect their bottom line."

HEAD GAMES

When 20-year-old Bowen Byram stepped away from Colorado in mid-January of 2022, you can be sure that hoisting a Stanley Cup six months later wasn't the first thing on his mind.

Byram was dealing with the lingering effects of his third documented concussion in less than a year. He had played five consecutive games after returning to the lineup from a six-game absence in December after sustaining concussion number three.

What followed was unexpected. The Avalanche granted Byram a personal leave and he returned to his family home in British Columbia to get himself right. That time off would end up being three months.

"It sucked, especially the start of January. I really started to feel not great," Byram told the *Denver Post*. "That's frustrating. I had already been out of the lineup two or three times with different issues. This one felt different, though. It wasn't going to be quick, and at that point in time I had no interest in playing hockey. I just wanted to get better."

Byram wasn't alone with his concussion issues. He was just one of twenty-five documented concussions in the 2021–22 season, although that number was probably significantly higher. As mentioned earlier, the prevalence of the upper body/lower body injury reporting has really muddied the waters. Many concussions are now being referred to as upper body or head injuries, with the truth often not coming out until a player speaks to the media after returning to the lineup.

According to NHL Injury Viz, the high-water mark for concussions in recent years was fifty-five in 2018–19, followed by forty-one in 2017–18, and thirty-four in 2019–20.

"Acceleration is often what produces injuries such as concussions. If you accelerate your head very quickly, the brain inside will experience a bigger acceleration and may suffer more damage than at a slower speed. It's the same thing during a collision between two vehicles," explains professor Alain Haché from the University of Moncton.

"Let's say you have a very heavy truck and a smaller, much lighter car. If there's a collision the force will be the same. But inside the car, the acceleration or deceleration will be much higher than in the truck. In the truck you won't feel much, but in the car you'll feel a huge change of speed, and that will cause injuries. The relative velocity is what matters. Whether one is moving, or the other isn't, or they both are, it's the difference of relative velocity that is important."

Once considered an issue dealt with primarily by the fighters, skill players in hockey are also being affected. Among the twenty-five players diagnosed in 2021–22, the list included Jonathan Toews, Tyler Johnson, Pavel Buchnevich, and Ondrej Kase.

In the case of Kase, it is becoming an all too familiar sight to see his name on the yearly lists.

In a seven-year career marred with multiple concussions, Kase missed another 20 games with Toronto in 2021–22. Add this to the 28 games he missed over two seasons in Anaheim, and the 53 on the sidelines with Boston in 2020–21, and it's safe to call the feisty forward concussion-prone. (Of course, those 53 games with Boston were listed as upper body on the team's injury report.)

One person who has been very outspoken about the NHL and concussions is Chris Nowinski, the co-founder and CEO of the Concussion Legacy Foundation, a non-profit organization leading the fight against concussions and CTE and dedicated to improving the lives of those impacted.

Chronic traumatic encephalopathy (CTE) is a progressive brain condition believed to be caused by repeated head blows and multiple episodes of concussions.

A former WWE wrestler whose career ended with a concussion, Nowinski says there are so many elements of hockey that make the players prone to concussion situations.

"CTE has been considered a fighter issue because some of the early cases were prominent fighters. But we've also diagnosed it in players who were known to be skilled players. I don't think there's an appreciation for the fact that the impacts in ice hockey are larger than they are in other sports, because skaters are traveling faster than people who run. You also have the ice surface and the boards that create more serious collisions than falling on turf or grass."

While Nowinski says there are some "weaknesses" in the NHL's concussion spotting and return to play protocols, his biggest concerns lie with the league's reluctance to acknowledge the connection between concussions and CTE.

For years now, NHL commissioner Gary Bettman has repeatedly denied any direct link between hockey-related concussions and a CTE diagnosis. However, a Boston University study of the brains of fourteen former NHL players determined that thirteen of them were found to have CTE. Among the players tested were Stan Mikita, Rick Martin, Steve Montador, Bob Probert, and Ralph Backstrom.

The news of Backstrom's diagnosis came less than a year after Andrew Shaw was forced to retire from the NHL on the advice of his doctors after suffering multiple concussions over his 10-year career with the Chicago Blackhawks and Montreal Canadiens.

"The NHL is doing a major disservice to hockey by claiming that they don't believe NHL play is or hockey play in general is linked to developing CTE. There's very clear cause and effect between repetitive head impacts and CTE," says Nowinski.

"So whether you're a boxer or football player, or soccer player or an ice hockey player, or in some situations in the NHL when a hockey player is also a boxer on skates, it's just absurd to still claim that hits to the head don't cause CTE and then align this policy of the sport to continue to put players in danger when reforms could be made."

JACK EICHEL SURGERY

One of the NHL's most high-profile soap operas in 2021 may have resulted in a major medical breakthrough for years to come.

For eight mind-numbing months, the hockey world watched as the relationship between Buffalo captain Jack Eichel and the franchise that selected him second overall in 2015 deteriorated by the day.

While some would say the breakup was inevitable, Eichel's disenchantment with the Sabres was only exacerbated by their inability to let him have the surgery of his choice.

It all started on March 7 when the Sabres faced the New York Islanders. Late in the game on Long Island, Eichel was battling with Casey Cizikas behind the net when he took a couple of hits along the boards from the Islanders forward. Moments later, Eichel could be seen on the bench in obvious discomfort while moving his head and neck around.

Eichel was diagnosed with a herniated disk a few days later, and he was eventually ruled out for the rest of the season on April 14. This is when things started to go south.

Since it is common for time to heal an injured disk, the Sabres hoped that rest and rehab would get the disk back in place, avoiding any kind of surgery. The two parties agreed that they'd revisit the conversation at the end of June. Both sides agreed that if there wasn't any improvement in Eichel's condition by then, surgery would be the next step.

Eichel wanted to have disk replacement surgery, but the Sabres doctors insisted on a disk fusion procedure. Since nobody in the NHL had ever undergone disk replacement surgery, the Sabres didn't want their 80 million dollar captain being a medical test run. With the NHL's collective bargaining agreement giving the team final say in all medical decisions, Eichel was at the mercy of the team's doctors.

Disk fusion is a procedure formally known as anterior cervical discectomy and fusion. The damaged disk is removed by cutting a hole in the front of the neck. From there, the bone is fused to the bone below, decreasing pressure from the nerve and helping stabilize the spinal cord. Former NFL MVP Peyton Manning is among the high-profile athletes that have had the procedure, and he played four more seasons afterwards.

The biggest downside to disk fusion is that the recovery period can be as long as ten months. And without a disk in place, more stress is placed on different levels of the neck and spine. With the motion of neck and spine often affected in the area where the disk was removed, it's also not uncommon for future discomfort and additional surgeries to occur.

Eichel's preferred method of disk replacement surgery is relatively new, having only been performed in the United States since 2000.

Just like it sounds, this involves replacing the damaged disk with an artificial motion device. Studies have shown that not only does this remove pressure from the nerve, it allows neck and spine motion to normalize without any added stress. Most importantly, the recovery time is typically in the three- to five-month range.

Complicating matters was the lack of information about professional athletes and disk replacement surgery. At that time, UFC fighter Chris Weidman was the highest-profile case of an athlete receiving disk replacement. Weidman went under the knife in January 2019, and returned to the octagon in August 2020.

The June deadline came and went, and the surgery stalemate dragged on through the summer. Eichel would ultimately fail his training camp physical in September, and was also stripped of his captaincy. A reported discussion between the two sides in October went nowhere, leaving a frustrated Eichel to continue playing the waiting game.

Everything finally came to a head on November 4 when Buffalo found the trading partner they'd been looking for, sending Eichel to Vegas for Alex Tuch, Peyton Krebs, and a pair of draft picks. Most importantly for Eichel, the Golden Knights had agreed to the disk replacement surgery he so desperately wanted.

Eichel underwent ADR surgery on November 12 at the Rocky Mountain Spine Clinic in Denver, with the seventy-five-minute procedure performed by Dr. Chad Prusmack, who is also a consultant to the NFL's Denver Broncos.

It didn't take long for Eichel to get back on the ice. Social media was buzzing just three weeks later when a short video clip of Eichel skating in full equipment went viral.

Staying true to the recovery timeline, Eichel practiced in full for the first time with his new teammates on January 11 and made his season debut at home against Colorado on February 16—just over three months after the surgery.

Eichel finished the season with 14 goals and 25 points in 34 games and averaged 19 minutes of ice time per game. Most importantly, the ADR surgery was never an issue, as Eichel didn't miss any games in his return.

Not unlike how Tommy John surgery has changed the game of baseball, disk replacement surgery could follow a similar path in a contact-heavy sport like hockey. Teams now have a template to work with in Eichel, potentially creating a more positive resolution to medical standoffs going forward. Not to mention, a quicker recovery time is appealing to all parties involved, especially if it's for one of the league's brightest stars.

The NHL's current CBA is set to expire on September 15, 2026, and you can almost guarantee that this will be one of the issues that will be discussed at length during negotiations of a new agreement.

10

TRAINING & FITNESS

Gary Roberts had an NHL career that most players would be jealous of. He played 21 seasons with six different teams from 1987 to 2009, won a Stanley Cup with Calgary in 1989, and scored 438 goals and 909 points over 1,224 games.

But it took a serious injury to start him on the road to becoming one of the most sought-after trainers in the hockey world.

It was during his time in Calgary where the rugged power forward developed bone spurs and nerve damage in his neck that affected his arm function, limiting him to just 43 games over two seasons from 1994 to 1996. Roberts required two surgeries to relieve the nerve impingement that eventually gave him full use of his arm, and he returned to score 22 goals in 35 games for the Flames.

When the neck pain continued, Roberts made the difficult decision to retire from the NHL in June of 1996 at the age of 30.

It was in the early stages of his retirement when Roberts discovered a passion for training. While working with his doctors in rehab, Roberts made the decision to revamp his workout routine. He overhauled his entire lifestyle and became consumed with learning more about fitness. This also led to Roberts returning to the NHL where he played 13 more seasons before retiring for good in 2009. His career would come full circle, as his last game was in Calgary on March 1, 2009, while playing for Tampa Bay.

Roberts, who also works as a Sports Performance Consultant with Seattle, credits his time in Pittsburgh and Tampa Bay with developing his passion to help younger players improve, both on and off the ice. He served as a mentor to Steven Stamkos, who was the number one overall pick in the 2008 NHL Draft and an

18-year-old rookie with Tampa Bay during Roberts's final season. The Toronto natives worked out together that summer and Roberts's love for personal training just snowballed from there.

"Rick Tocchet was coaching Tampa at that time, and he asked me if I could train with Steve in the summertime. We both live in the Toronto area (Stamkos in Markham, Roberts in nearby Uxbridge), and I had just retired.

"For me having that opportunity to train with Stammer, just me and him that summer, that's when I fell in love with what I do. I gave him the information and he did the work. He still puts in the work to this day. It's been exciting to watch."

In 2011, Roberts put his passion to work when he opened up the Gary Roberts High Performance Training Center. Located just north of Toronto, it's become the summertime epicenter for NHL players to train during the offseason.

Stamkos is part of a crew that returns to the GRHPTC each summer for the legendary twelve-week regimen of fitness and lifestyle training. Edmonton superstar and two-time NHL MVP Connor McDavid grew up not far away from the complex and has been a regular since he was a teenager.

When he was a youngster in the program, McDavid always made a point of working out in the same group with Stamkos, who is seven years his elder. McDavid saw the impact the training had on Stamkos's career and wanted to compete at that level.

As the years have gone on, Stamkos insists on having Roberts place him in the same group as the now 25-year-old McDavid. Coming off a career-high 106 points in 2021–22 at age 32, Stamkos seems to have found the strategy to find the fountain of youth.

In the summer of 2021, some of the notable participants included Gabriel Landeskog (Colorado), Darnell Nurse (Edmonton), Zach Hyman (Edmonton), Brandon Tanev (Seattle), Chris Tanev (Calgary), Chris Tierney (Calgary), and Josh Anderson (Montreal).

This isn't just a bunch of guys showing up to the local gym to get in a good sweat each day. From the moment the players arrive, they are treated in world-class fashion in a manner that basically mimics their in-season routine.

"When they come to us in the summer, they get treated like they're at a first-class NHL facility, no different than how things are run in places like Pittsburgh, Toronto, or Vegas. They get breakfast when they arrive in the morning, followed by treatment if they need it," Roberts explains.

"From there it's time for the workout that we have prescribed specifically for them. After that it's time for a good stretch or even some yoga. They'll have another meal before they leave and also grab some of the healthy snacks we offer for later on. A guy that typically arrives by seven thirty in the morning will likely be with us for about three to four hours each day."

Long gone are the days of players using the summer to workout, relax, and just rest their bodies, while getting in the occasional skate. The program is offered five days a week, and then on weekends depending on if a guy that needs a little more aerobic activity or some additional mobility work.

Roberts meets with each attendee individually before they start the program to review their season and discuss their goals for summer training.

First and foremost, it's about the player's current health. Before they can begin planning a program, Roberts needs to understand where the individual is at physically. Are they still getting over an injury, and if so, what's their current performance level? Each player will go through a battery of tests to determine what's right for them in that moment. They will also be evaluated again at the beginning of each week.

These discussions will also talk about any specific on-ice performance issues that a player wants to be resolved. Some guys, like Landeskog in the summer of 2021, just want to improve their foot speed because they feel like they've lost a step.

Roberts had a proud papa moment the next season. While watching an Avalanche game on television, he heard one of the commentators mention how the 28-year-old Landeskog had clearly done some work in the offseason because he was noticeably quicker.

"It means a lot when a guy of Gabe's stature comes in and trusts us with his health and training. And then to see him get the results he was looking for makes it even more satisfying."

Others want to get stronger in order to win more battles and be harder on the puck. If a player simply wants to improve his shot, Roberts will create a plan that not only strengthens the hands and wrists, he'll create a workout that makes their rotational core strength stronger too.

There's no one-size-fits-all approach to training, and Roberts says that's even more important as it relates to hockey.

"Hockey is one of the toughest sports to train for because you need a little of everything. You need strength, first and foremost. Then you need to be able to access that strength through your power and your speed. But then you need to be agile. And then you need to be quick. But you still need to have endurance.

"I know that you can't accomplish all this in just twelve weeks of training. My goal is to make a player leave here feeling better than they did when we started. It's also about helping a guy learn more about his body and giving them an opportunity to play at a high level for a very long time."

The summer program offers options for players of all ages and abilities, with the majority being teens and older. Roberts and his team of trainers build specific programming for each phase of the program that targets a player's individual needs and injury history. While some of the NHL players may only come for a few weeks to kick-start their own workout programs, others will do the entire twelve weeks that is divided into different steps.

It starts with the general prep and health phase that's aimed at getting someone in the general state to train hard. If someone arrives without any nagging injury issues, they will probably go through this in three to four weeks.

The true strength power phase involves workouts like pushing heavy sleds, lifting heavy weights, and doing plenty of plyometric work that uses speed and force to build muscle power. Roberts says the only way to do any of this is if you're completely healthy, or there's a risk of injury. After that it's about getting the speed up and preparing for game-playing mode.

"For some players, they truthfully don't ever get to that stage where they're able to be in there for a period of time to make a difference. On the NHL side, most of them are too beat up to do all twelve weeks. The NHL season is long and grinding, I know that. Our goal at that point is just trying to keep them healthy and get them through another year. Hopefully at the end of the next year, we'll have a better opportunity to work on some stuff."

Roberts believes that one of the most important parts of his training happens away from the gym. It's his goal to work with the younger players to help them fully grasp what a healthy lifestyle can do for your future, just like it changed his own trajectory after the neck injury that nearly cut his career short.

It's not just the weights and training that matter to Roberts. He takes a holistic approach to the entire process, truly believing in lifestyle, nutrition, hydration, and sleep as being the core foundation of a player's development.

For the veteran NHLers that attend his summer program, much of this behavior has become second nature to them, especially if they are planning on a long, successful career. That's why Roberts spends extra time with the younger players to teach them the ideals and values that can get them started on the path to professional success.

"They need to understand it's not all about what happens on the ice. When you're away from the rink at night, are you putting your phone away and sipping on water? Are you getting the eight to ten hours of sleep that a young athlete needs? And are you getting up at eight in the morning and having a really healthy one-thousand-calorie breakfast to get your day started?

"The player that does it the way that I hope he will, is going to have a better chance at longevity than the player that's going to bed well after midnight and eating a crappy breakfast and grabbing a coffee on his way to the rink."

FOOD FOR THOUGHT

Speaking as a father who can barely plan meals for a family of three, I can only imagine the kind of time and effort that has to go into Lisa McDowell's job as the team nutritionist for the Detroit Red Wings.

Now in her thirteenth season with the Red Wings, McDowell is responsible for carefully designing all the meals consumed by the players throughout the season. This includes breakfast, lunch, pregame, and postgame both home and away, along with everything served on the team's charter airplane when the Red Wings hit the road.

This isn't just about food prep for a team of hungry athletes. McDowell also keeps a close eye on what supplements are being used, such as plant and whey protein, fish oils, Omega-3, and Vitamin D.

McDowell also plays a part in the sports science aspect of nutrition, as the team does a comprehensive blood panel on each player at the beginning of the season. Her role as a nutritionist is to make sure each player has good blood sugar control in order to maximize the glycogen stores, which help maintain an individual's energy level and their ability to perform to the max ability.

"I need to make sure that the guys are optimized on paper by monitoring the readings for things like Vitamin D and cortisol for stress, testosterone for hormones, creatine kinase for muscle damage, and C reactive protein for inflammation."

Her job doesn't stop when the final buzzer goes. McDowell meets with each player individually to design an offseason plan for target body composition. Whether it's managing weight gain, weight maintenance, or leaning out, it's her job to keep a watchful eye on each player to ensure they arrive at training camp the next season in the best shape possible.

McDowell's duties aren't limited to the players on the NHL roster. When Detroit hosts their summer development camp for younger prospects and recently drafted players, McDowell spends a considerable amount of time teaching them cooking and lifestyle strategies that will help them thrive going forward.

"We do a lot of hands-on education and cooking classes. I team up with our chef, and we teach the guys how to use a knife, how to grocery shop, how to read a food label, and what to eat when they eat out at restaurants. And then some very simple recipes that don't even need a written recipe, using food they just can assemble with things they would normally have on hand."

McDowell says that the cooking skills really vary from player to player depending on where they came from or how they were raised. With so many players having lived at billet houses in junior hockey or dorm rooms in college, they may or not have much experience when it comes to shopping and preparing for meals.

But then there are guys like 22-year-old forward Joe Veleno who benefitted from his mother's teachings as a youngster and really hit the ground running when it came to cooking for himself.

Because of the hockey lifestyle at all levels that involves morning practices and considerable travel, it's important for players to be eating healthy as much as possible, and not relying on fast food and coffee to keep them fueled.

"Most of the young guys really liked the cooking strategies and understood how important they are. Knowing they are on a tight schedule, we teach them how to batch cook once or twice a week, with a lot of the shopping being done at Costco because we want them buying in bulk. So they're making things like overnight oats with a plant-based milk for the week, along with a sheet pan of roasted veggies, and Buddha bowls."

McDowell explains that the bowl strategy is an easy way for young players to learn how to eat properly. A well-constructed Buddha bowl has five essential elements: protein, grains, at least two vegetables, a healthy fat like an avocado for supporting hormones, and a "sprinkle" that is some form of nuts or seeds. It's this commonsense approach to eating that shows the players that cooking doesn't have to be complicated.

Knowing that there are certain foods that impact that inflammation pathway, McDowell says they are always working with the young players on constructing their shopping lists and everyday eating habits, while also understanding there needs to be affordable options. This could be something as simple as using frozen blueberries in their smoothies, so that the fresh blueberries never go bad. Blueberries are chock-full of vitamins and antioxidants called flavonoids that can help reduce inflammation.

"Once you get to the big show and we're cooking for you on an almost daily basis, it's pretty easy. It's more of a gladiator approach because everything is there. But the young guys don't have the benefit of that. The more we teach them early on, it can only help going forward. And we understand that it's important to teach them how to do it affordably."

As is commonplace with the majority of NHL teams, the Detroit roster is a collection of players from all over the world. Detroit's young core of emerging young stars features 2021–22 Calder Trophy winner Moritz Seider (Germany), forward Lucas Raymond (Sweden), and defenseman Filip Hronek (Czech Republic). They are led by a veteran core that includes a pair of 30-goal scorers in captain Dylan Larkin (United States) and forward Tyler Bertuzzi (Canada).

One of the challenges that McDowell has faced throughout her career is learning the cultural preferences for food of these various countries. Not only does she work with the team's chef to bring a bite of home to various meals when possible, she wants to always be working with the players to expand their palates. But it all has to be done with a specific plan in mind.

"It's important to let them eat something they enjoy, but it needs to be done in a healthy manner. We don't always do it better in America, especially if you look around at the obesity rates. I really need to teach the guys what is a garbage product, how to read labels, and what to stay away from.

"We are a very whole food, plant-forward team. I'm not saying we're vegan or plant-based, but we make sure that all of those polyphenols and phytochemicals are on the plate of every player and that they have access to foods that contain nitrate like spinach, and beets for the oxygen advantage."

Polyphenols are powerful antioxidants commonly referred to "lifespan essentials" that can help avoid risk of chronic diseases. Studies have shown they can be beneficial to blood pressure levels and heart health, and can aid the immune system in fighting off infections. Foods such as berries, herbs and spices, cocoa powder, and nuts are among the highest in polyphenol content.

Originating from the Greek word *phyto* that means plant, phytochemicals are natural compounds found in plant-based foods. Not only do these compounds provide the characteristic taste and aroma, they act as the plant's immune system. By "eating a rainbow" of fruits, vegetables, nuts, and seeds, phytochemicals have the ability to improve the function of your immune system, reduce inflammation, and regulate hormones.

TAKEOUT OPTIONS

Making healthy grab and go options available in the locker room are also a priority for McDowell, especially after games. It can be very tempting for a player to be lured by a plate of chicken wings after a game in Buffalo, or a couple of the famous Bell Centre hot dogs in Montreal. (For the record, McDowell says those are two of the foods she actually allows in the locker room postgame when the team is on the road. She'll also bend the rules if some of Pat's cheesesteaks magically show up after a game in Philadelphia.)

When the Red Wings play at home, it's not uncommon to see players walking out of Little Caesars Arena with a pint of blueberries or raspberries to eat in the car on the way home. Instead of a postgame beer or two, McDowell says they also encourage players to pour themselves a cup of chamomile tea for the drive home so they can help shut it down and go to sleep easier.

DON'T SLEEP ON IT

In addition to being a registered dietitian, McDowell also has another credential through lifestyle medicine, which allows her to provide competent advice on best practices when it comes to other treatments of issues like sleep and stress management. These are two of the six pillars of lifestyle medicine that McDowell regularly references, along with the nutrition aspect. (The remaining three pillars? Physical activity, relationships, and tobacco cessation.)

It is important for her to provide the players with the micro and macro nutrients that support good sleep, stress management, and again, setting up those hormones to be as optimal as possible, and then connecting with how that fits with all of the other recovery modalities.

When it comes to sleep, McDowell included the best practices from researchers around the country in the lengthy sleep protocol that she prepared for the team. The thirty-two-page document touches on a number of important elements where proper sleep can be beneficial with the recovery process, including simple things like making their bedroom as comfortable as possible, both at home and on the road.

"When we're on the road, we give the players those little blackout dots to cover the light on the smoke detector because even that one little pinpoint of light can inhibit your melatonin production. We also encourage them to have the temperature set at sixty-six degrees, making their bedroom or hotel room feel like a cold, dark cave."

Players are also instructed to have their own covers, not to share the blankets with the significant others, sleep in layers, and keep their hands and feet untucked.

Even sleeping with a dog in the bed is frowned upon in McDowell's protocols, but she's aware that some people tend to sleep better when their dog is with them. While it may seem to be a trivial element, setting up the bedroom is one of the key strategies for good sleep hygiene.

Something else that McDowell monitors is the use of caffeine, encouraging players to only consume it on game days. McDowell refers to caffeine half-life, or how long it can remain in your system. Caffeine can reach a peak stimulant level in your blood within thirty to sixty minutes after consuming it, and it can linger for anywhere from three to five hours afterwards, but everyone is different. Some Detroit players have gone to the trouble of finding out if they're a slow or fast metabolizer and have used that infor-mation accordingly for their caffeine consumption.

Maintaining a consistent postgame snack routine is also a key contributor to how a player can successfully fall asleep. This includes consuming snacks like pistachios and almonds that are loaded with magnesium. Tart cherry juice is a popular postgame drink, as it helps reduce inflammation. Chamomile tea has also become a staple because it contains apigenin, an antioxidant that helps with muscle relaxation and sedation.

If kiwis are your thing, they are rich with serotonin and antioxidants and have proven to be very helpful when eaten before bed. Believe it or not, some players even eat them with the skin on for additional nutritional benefits.

Maintaining a consistent and successful sleep routine is so very important during the grind of an NHL season. With all the late-night flights, time zone changes, and morning skates, it can be very easy to slip into bad habits between the sheets.

"We educate them on the risk of injury when they're not getting enough sleep. Many of them use wearables. So we teach them how to interpret their data. So if they're short on deep sleep, if they're short on REM sleep, we provide the evidence-based strategies on how to remedy those two situations.

"The guys who use the wearable devices [such as the Oura ring] see how alcohol impacts their sleep. So that's been the best absolute observed tool for changing behavior there. And then we just look at some of the tricks that we've taught them, like being exposed to the blue light from a phone and not playing the killer video games, because they both increase your parasympathetic nervous system."

WINDING DOWN

The parasympathetic nervous system controls the stimulation of the "rest and digest" functions of the body while someone is at rest. Getting into this state is especially key after spending the day preparing the body to compete in a stressful activity like an NHL game for three hours. Even a beer league player knows how difficult it is to fall asleep when playing a late night game, and then having to get up for work the next day. Although, whacking a few beers in the locker room afterwards definitely won't make it any easier.

On non-game nights, McDowell suggests setting an alarm at a certain time each night to start the winddown routine. She also encourages reading a book in bed rather than watching movies or staying up late playing those shooter video games that can drive up the heart rate at a time of night when your body should be starting to relax.

Stress control is very important, so something as simple as laughing can be helpful at night. Some players turn to their phones for meditation and calming apps like Calm or Headspace to clear their head, and others have used the innovative Wim Hof Method breathing techniques created by a Dutch motivational speaker and extreme athlete.

With a good sleep routine playing such an important part in the NHL lifestyle, it's important to monitor it throughout the year. McDowell says that players that use the wearable devices have an advantage because it can help detect some possible red flags if they are having trouble sleeping.

"The wearables detect apnea episodes, and I really think sleep apnea is under-diagnosed in [the] NHL. If we notice any issue like that, where it just doesn't make sense that a guy's not sleeping, then we refer them to a sleep specialist because there are some things that are not within my scope. And if I can't get it fixed with a good sleep routine, then they go out for sleep studies."

11

ANALYTICS

Former Buffalo head coach Ted Nolan didn't exactly endear himself to the analytics community back in 2014. Speaking to the media following a training camp session, Nolan was asked about his thoughts on the growing analytics movement that had permeated the NHL in recent years. His response stunned a few in the room.

"The information I use is with my eyes and my soul and my heart. If I see someone who's competing and I know he's competing, that's good enough for me. I don't need a machine telling me how hard he worked. I can see it for myself."

It was actually a strange flex for Nolan because it came at a time when the Sabres and several other teams had started dipping their toes into the analytical waters.

This old-school way of thinking has permeated the NHL's old boy network for years, and likely explains why teams were so resistant to the twenty-first century's analytics invasion. Looking at the game through a fresh set of eyes using numbers never seen before just wasn't going to fly for many in the game.

Coaches, players, and executives already had video and conventional game stats at their disposal. Tried and true numbers like shots on goal, time on ice, and plus/minus were all they needed to review games and pre-scout the opposition. The advanced use of video had also been considered a big step for many teams, and the good old "eye test" was the gold standard for backing up their statistical analysis.

As the internet buzz continued to grow, and many hockey bloggers turned their hobbies into passion projects, the concept of advanced stats in hockey began to take hold. Analysts like Tyler Dellow and Eric Tulsky quickly grew their online presence and became as well known in hockey circles as the players themselves. These statistical pioneers were at the forefront of creating a new way to break down the game of hockey.

Whereas the traditional stats provided by the NHL's game-night crews serve as a snapshot in time, the purpose of advanced stats is to add another layer to those numbers. Creating quantifiable data over a period of time allows the user to identify trends, or simply study a specific game situation.

Using popular metrics like puck possession, zone entries, and five-on-five scoring, coaches and fans can look deeper into the game, often giving credence to a scenario they believed existed but had no discernible way to explain it in the moment.

But as the analytics movement strengthened among fans, the mainstream media was very resistant to the attention being given to these new methods of analyzing the game. Print and broadcast media that had been covering the game for years were basically ignoring analytics and their impact on the game. The media's staunch refusal to acknowledge these "fancy stats" became a point of contention in the industry.

The tide started to turn in 2014, affectionately known as the NHL's summer of analytical love. Despite the media's ignorance, several teams began giving public approval to analytics, even hiring some of the internet's biggest stars for front-office positions.

Dellow was hired by Edmonton before moving on to New Jersey. Carolina brought in Tulsky as their vice president of hockey management and strategy, and he's since been promoted to assistant general manager.

When the expansion Seattle Kraken began play in the 2021–22 season, they dove headfirst into the pool by creating one of the more robust analytics departments in the NHL. Alexandra Mandrycky oversees the group that includes Eric Mathiasen, a lifelong hockey fan who was working on cloud and artificial intelligence projects at Microsoft before joining the Kraken.

In an interview with *The Athletic* in December of 2020, Mathiasen reinforced the common belief among the analytics community that advanced stats help find additional meaning in some of the sport's traditional numbers.

"Analytics are not about telling the whole story. A player can have different statistics or heart that cannot be measured. Analytics are an important part of the story," he explains. "It's amazing to see the buy-in that we are getting and going from there and we're starting to look at these interesting analytical pieces and how they fit into the bigger picture."

There's always going to be people who are more accepting of analytics than others. And the reality of it is, analytics aren't meant to replace the expert-level experience and knowledge that a coach, manager, or player may have. They are meant to enhance.

Take a look at any industry, it doesn't even need to be anything that's related to sports at all. It would be laughable to think that people across all industries aren't using business analytics to gain some form of advantage.

Is it plausible to think that the CEO of a bank would just look at a business opportunity and say 'I'm just gonna go with my gut'? Not a chance. They'll take every piece of valuable information they have at their disposal to make the most informed decision possible. And that's all analytics is. It doesn't replace anything, it simply adds another useful layer to the decision-making process.

PRESENT DAY

The analytics train continues to roll through NHL front offices, adding new passengers at breakneck pace.

Back in July 2019, *The Athletic* reported on the number of analytical hires listed for each of the thirty-one teams at that time. The list totaled fifty-three names over twenty-seven teams, with only Anaheim, Minnesota, the Islanders, and St. Louis lacking any form of analytics staffers.

In a follow-up report in June 2022, that list had grown exponentially to 118, and all thirty-two teams were represented. The most robust group is based in Toronto, as the Maple Leafs list eight people in their analytics department, and that doesn't include their number-crunching general manager, Kyle Dubas.

This collection of data hounds also doesn't take into account the independent contractors hired by teams, including companies like Sportlogiq, Stathletes, and Clear Sight Analytics, run by former NHL goaltender and current MSG Network analyst Steve Valiquette.

But when it comes to finding out exactly what teams are using the numbers for, there is no definitive answer because nobody really wants to tip their hand. Multiple teams and organizations were contacted to be interviewed for this project, and they either ignored the request or politely declined it.

Knowing how razor-thin the margins are between winning and losing in pro sports, it shouldn't really come as a surprise how protective these teams are. The whole idea behind investing in analytics is so that you can gain any kind of microscopic edge on your competitors, so it's the last thing they'll want to discuss it in any great detail, if at all.

Some teams are using analytics across all aspects of the organization, including things that are removed from the playing surface like ticket sales and marketing initiatives. Others are just applying them to hockey-related events like the entry draft and talent acquisition, using the data to help identify the right players for the right roles.

Analytics have become an important role in all forms of business. But as they pertain to hockey, some teams are using them really effectively in key areas, while others are still trying to find their way out of the shallow end.

PROSPECT MINING

One area of hockey operations that has seen a significant use of analytics is amateur scouting, and helping to identify prospects for the annual entry draft.

The human performance side of things is obviously an area where data is important. If you really think about it, the draft combine is all about analytics. It's about gathering as much data as you can about each prospect.

There are just a multitude of statistical approaches that teams would use to measure talent to prepare for the draft. For each general manager it's all about decision-making and wanting to feel like they've got some support or resources that help make what is a very difficult job just a little bit easier.

This is particularly relevant when you're talking about drafting kids who are still just 17 and 18 years old. Prospects in hockey are drafted younger than any other sport, so it's important for general managers to have as much data and support as possible.

At the conclusion of the 2022 draft in Montreal, Buffalo's director of amateur scouting, Jerry Forton, explained to the media how the team uses the analytics data to complement the viewings of players by their scouting staff.

By combining the two resources, Forton and his team worked with general manager Kevyn Adams to put together their final list of prospects. Forton even went out of his way to recognize the work of Sam Ventura, Buffalo's vice president of hockey strategy and research.

"Every year, the list seems to get more and more exact. Every single name in our top 130 went off the board in the first six rounds. There were years previous where you could get through the draft with eighty, ninety, or one hundred names at the most. The whole league is getting better at identifying players, and I've said how useful our analytics staff is for us early on—especially at the mid-year point—of making sure we're getting proper coverage of all players.

"They do a great job of steering our amateur staff when we're not getting enough looks, live or on video, of players. When we have a disparity, especially at the top of the draft between what the analytics staff is seeing and what the amateur staff is seeing with their eyes, we've got to get to the bottom of that pretty quickly. You certainly don't want to be calling a name in the top two or three rounds where there's a disconnect."

ORGANIZATIONAL THEORY

By all accounts, there is a general overall acceptance within organizations that analytics are important in that they should at least be a part of the decision-making process, which was definitely not the case, even a short time ago.

Having said that, there's a wide breadth of integration across different organizations, at the professional level in terms of how well and how much they're being integrated. Not to mention how much teams are investing in them and how successful they've been at implementing them into the decision-making process.

Watching a team like Seattle go all in so quickly was an interesting—and very public—case study. The Kraken made no secret of their plans to use analytics in not only helping build their expansion team from scratch, but it also in their search for a general manager that ultimately resulted in the hiring of Ron Francis.

If there were teams out there that were hesitant to make the investment, Dominic Moore said you can be sure there were a lot of people paying close attention to how things have worked out for the Kraken so far.

"Some might say, 'they were so heavily invested in analytics and look what it got them.' [Seattle was thirtieth in the NHL in their expansion season with a record of 27–49–6.] But there are so many different aspects to success in an organization that go beyond the data, as important as the data is. Vegas clearly embraces and is empowered by their analytics approach, and it's worked for them. At the end of the day you can argue it both ways. But I think it's like any managerial problem. Things are done well or, or they're not in, you know, there's a spectrum there where some things are done well, and others aren't. And it's always hard to put everything together. Being a GM is a really hard thing."

There's also a fine line teams need to walk with analytics when it comes to the players, especially the ones that haven't exactly embraced the movement yet. If you've ever seen the 2011 movie *Moneyball*, think back to the utterly confused looks on the players' faces as the characters played by Brad Pitt (Billy Beane) and Jonah Hill (Peter Brand) were explaining detailed statistical information to them for the first time.

As a stats guy himself, Moore appreciates the role that numbers play in sports. Analytics weren't even an issue when he made his NHL debut in 2003, but they were gaining momentum when he retired following the 2018 season. Ironically, his last stop was in Toronto, one of the teams that has invested heavily in analytics almost from day one.

Moore says every player is different when it comes to stats, and in some cases, too much information can be a bad thing for some guys.

"I think it really runs the gamut for the players and how accepting they are of analytics. Some just don't want any part of it, they just want to play the game the way they've always played it using the statistics they are familiar with.

"Then there are others who might use it as a tool to self-assess and find areas of weakness or areas that they've tried to improve on, because every player's trying to figure that out. But there are some players who look at it like they're being graded by their coaches and managers with too much scrutiny and it really affects them negatively."

GREAT EXPECTATIONS

If there's one thing we've come to learn about sports, it's that the numbers may not paint a complete picture of an athlete's overall ability, especially at an exact moment in time in their career.

A power hitter in baseball could be in a prolonged slump, putting a damper on his home run and RBI totals. He still appears to be making solid contact, but he just can't find the holes or avoid the gloves on defense. Even though his production rates are way down, chances are his hard-hit rates and exit velocity numbers haven't been affected. In layman's terms, he's doing everything right but just can't catch a break.

In hockey, the analytics crowd refers to these as expected goals.

The most important thing in a game is goals. If you score more than your opponent, you win. Everybody knows that. From there, you look at expected goals, which is just a goal probability of the shot attempts that you generated in that game. That will be the process underneath the result. And it doesn't always match because a team can wildly outplay another team, but one goalie steals a game. But it just helps you understand how your team performs. So you go from goals to expected goals.

As Mike Kelly likes to say, expected goals are just another one of those analytical onions with multiple layers. As you start peeling the onion, you can uncover more elements of play.

"Peel the onion, another layer, and you can start to break down how you created that goal probability based on your shot attempts. Were you able to outchance your opponent off the rush by cycling the puck by for checking rebounds in front of the net? Beyond that, you can start looking at the location of different shots as well. To understand where you were able to get shots from, was it from quality areas, was it from one area of the ice versus another?"

One example Kelly referred to was a game between Pittsburgh and Boston on April 21, 2022. Pittsburgh won the game, 4–0, but were outshot by Boston 52–32—including a 41–19 margin over the final two periods. Not surprisingly, the headline for the game recap on NHL.com was "DeSmith has 52-save shutout; Penguins defeat Bruins to gain in Metro."

There's no denying Pittsburgh goalie Casey DeSmith his 52 save performance; that shutout will forever be part of his career stats. But a closer look at the numbers revealed that only three of the Boston shots came from the most dangerous area on the ice, which is the front inner slot region known as the "home plate area."

This desirable scoring region on the ice is defined as a line across the top of the faceoff circles, down to the faceoff dots, and then diagonally into the crease.

Noted Kelly, "That's a tremendous job by Pittsburgh in their own zone to keep the Bruins out of the dangerous scoring areas for the most part, and it makes the goalie's night much easier when the shots aren't as difficult. So it's really to me it's just about peeling the layers back farther and farther and farther to understand the game. From a process standpoint in as much detail as you can. From high-level, you obviously look at goals from now to go right to expected goals. And from that I go into how did they create that goal probability in the game?"

When it comes to expected goals in hockey, we are talking about a player who hasn't scored but has a high expected goal total within a certain period of time based on where his scoring chances are coming from. It's a reflection that they're absolutely getting quality opportunities, but just can't convert.

So then you grab one of Kelly's onions and start peeling the layers back. Is he getting the chances or not? If the answer is yes, then you're less concerned. But if he's not, then you have every right to start blowing him up on Twitter and making those outrageously hot takes on sports radio shows that everyone loves so much.

This is where the role of the hockey fan comes into play. There can be a little bit of an underestimation—especially from certain portions of the media—as to how intelligent the fans are, how much research they do on their own, and the types of information that they're interested in. And especially in this day and age, there's a lot of really educated fans, and they expect their coverage to be as informative as possible.

"It's all part of the storytelling. Again, that's where I think this information is really critical. As I said before, you don't have to make it this simply into an analytics thing," says Kelly. "If you're an analyst or a writer or just a guy talking to his buddy, you use the numbers to help you tell a complete story of what is happening on the ice. Not only do fans understand this information, they want more of it."

BENCH PERSPECTIVE

Even though the earlier example of the statement made by Ted Nolan is nearly a decade old, it's still uncertain what kind of impact analytics have made on NHL coaches. From the people I spoke with, it's definitely not a straight line.

That being said, if you just listen to press conferences, you'll hear coaches talk about how a line performed against another line, they'll refer to expected goals, and their volume of scoring chances. It's clear that some are paying attention, but how it impacts decision-making will change from coach to coach.

In his role with Sportlogiq, Kelly has made presentations to large groups of coaches at both the NHL and junior levels, and worked one on one with many others. He's discovered that once a coach understands how to make the data work in their favor, they want to know more.

"What I find interesting is that the people that tend to seek out this type of information are often the people that we would look at as being highly successful. And you could think to yourself, 'Well, they're so good already. What do they need this for?' I believe part of the reason why anybody is great at anything is they're always looking to get better, and it's usually the top performers that are the ones reaching out trying to find ways to get even better.

"I've worked with coaches on understanding, with as much granularity as possible, how their team is performing, the trends of the game, studying opponents, and where they can find those little slight edges. And there are ways to make this information actionable to help improve performance."

Kelly shared an example of his recent work with someone who was coaching at a high level of hockey. This coach already understood what areas of the game that the successful playoff teams typically excelled in, but he wanted to go deeper into the numbers.

From his experience behind the bench, the one area that the coach wanted to really key in on with Kelly was a team's ability to perform in the neutral zone. The coach knew how critical it was to have the ability to deny entries into your zone, deny successful possession plays into your zone, and get the puck out and transition it up the ice.

Neutral-zone play was something this coach understood from a kind of a commonsense perspective, but Kelly said that being able to look at actual numbers and really see how valuable they were to his research was a bit of an eye-opener for the coach.

"For him, it was just in terms of better understanding how good the best teams are in controlling that neutral-zone area. My goal was to help him make this information actionable based on his experience and knowledge. With more information at his disposal, the coach is now able to develop strategies to make sure that his team is able to disrupt those entries, and then use that opportunity to be able to quickly move the puck up the ice and attack with speed."

Having more information is never a bad thing. Maybe this new nugget of information will change how much time the coach will now dedicate to working on this in practice. That probably never crossed his mind when he first started the project.

There's a lot of ways for coaches to try and use the information and analytics to understand the key parts of the game with as much detail as possible. It's stuff that coaches have done for years. But the information is now available in real time and in more detail than it ever has been.

LEARNING ON THE FLY

Analytics weren't even a thing when Dave Barr first stepped behind an NHL bench in 2008. So as time went on and the data slowly started trickling in to his daily conversations at the rink, you could probably forgive him for not wanting to hear any of this outside noise.

That wasn't the case at all.

Barr understood that if he wanted to be successful, he needed to keep an open mind to new thoughts and ideas when it came to how hockey was being analyzed and dissected. If the game was changing and evolving, then it was up to him to do the same.

"You've really gotta roll with it and accept it. I actually think some of the data is kind of fun to use," says Barr. "The eye test is still very much part of it, but you have to be open to learning. Pretty much every coach is open to that, whether it's a little bit or a lot, everybody is and understanding that it helps. The data definitely helps, that's for sure."

Barr found the information particularly useful while he was running special teams units in San Jose, New Jersey, and Minnesota. Even after watching hours of video, Barr learned firsthand that some of the data he was given was helping him discover things that he wasn't recognizing in his viewings.

For instance, oftentimes if he'd notice that the zone entries on a power play weren't going smoothly, Barr would just write it off to the personnel that were on the ice, or assumed the defenders were doing a great job of cutting off the lanes.

"Then I'd find out that we had a 75 percent entry rate on the right side, as opposed to a 60 percent entry on the left side with the exact same group. You don't let the numbers dictate exactly what you're going to do, you just keep that in your head going forward. You have to be careful how you utilize the analytics that are provided to you."

CREASE CRASHING

It's always been fairly simple to judge a goalie based on their stats. In terms of the traditional statistics, you have the goals against average, which is highly team performance-dependent. And then you have save percentage, which doesn't factor in the quality of the shot at all.

According to Kelly, that's exactly why we need analytics to fairly evaluate a goaltender's performance. It's not perfect by any means, but it's more accurate than just saying a goalie had a .905 save percentage, because again, that doesn't account for shot quality.

If a pass comes from behind the goal line and a forward one-times it from right in front of the net, it's likely that shot has a much higher goal probability than a shot from the point would. But you wouldn't know the difference just by looking at the save percentage.

"That is exactly why we need analytics with goaltending. So when we look at goals saved above expected, it factors in the probability of that shot going into the expected goal total for that shot," explains Kelly. "And then it at least more fairly evaluates the goaltender based on the quality of the shots that he faced."

Using Vancouver's Demko as a current example, Kelly points out that he has solid traditional numbers in terms of goals against average and save percentage. But when you factor in that over the past couple of seasons, the Canucks have allowed a pretty high degree of dangerous scoring chances against, it doesn't accurately reflect him as what he is, someone who Kelly believes is one of the best goalies in the NHL.

Conversely, there are goalies who play on really good defensive teams who put up really good save percentage and goals against numbers. But when you look at goals saved versus expected, their numbers aren't quite as good. That stat factors in shot quality, which is an essential part of evaluating a goaltender.

To better illustrate this, let's look at Philipp Grubauer's past two seasons.

In his 2020–21 season with Colorado, he was a Vezina Trophy finalist with a record of 30–9–1, and he posted an exceptional goals against average of 1.95 along with a .922 save percentage. That season, the Avalanche also happened to be the best defensive team in the league in terms of expected goals against, meaning the best team defense in front of a goalie.

Grubauer left the Avs to sign as a free agent with the expansion Seattle Kraken, where he no longer had the luxury of playing behind the league's top defensive team. As a result, his numbers (3.16, .889) suffered a little bit with the new team.

The Grubauer example may be a bit extreme, but it speaks volumes to Kelly's point about the true definition of the statistics.

"That's just again, trying to understand how much of a goalie's traditional statistics are team-influenced versus their own individual performance. Again, it's not perfect. But it just goes to show exactly why we need analytics to effectively evaluate goaltenders to the best of our ability."

DISRUPTION JUNCTION

During my six seasons working in public relations in Buffalo, one of my main responsibilities each night was to manage the game-night operations of the press box. In addition to making sure there was always enough coffee on hand for the media, I also had to coordinate the distribution of game statistics at each intermission.

Copies of the NHL's official game summary and event summary had to delivered to all the broadcast booths, TV trucks, and, most importantly, the coaches' offices for both teams.

Both documents contain all the relevant smorgasbord of game stats including the scoring summary, list of penalties, special teams numbers, shots on goal, and faceoffs. The event summary is the more thorough of the two, as it has all the players from both teams listed individually with a full breakdown of their stats. This is the one that most players look at closely to see why they weren't credited with more shots or hits. You know, all the things that matter come contract time.

There's no question each document serves its purpose as a hub for all the official stats being tracked and disseminated by the league's off-ice officials. But if you're a coach or broadcaster trying to dig deeper into what the numbers actually mean, they are really devoid of any true insight into how the game is truly being played out.

That's why Kelly thinks the time is "ripe for disruption" to start making changes to the presentation of game-night stats, at the both the league and broadcast levels.

"What you often see on an intermission graphic in terms of the game summary is goals, shots, faceoffs, hits, and blocked shots. Those are incredibly important. Shots don't have a meaningful correlation to winning or losing, but it's still something that I think should be included that the fans understand and are relevant.

"Hits, faceoffs and blocked shots actually have a very weak correlation to winning and sometimes a negative correlation to winning. So those three to me, should be off of the graphic if we want to talk about what actually matters in this game. There's better information available today that can help tell the story of the game in a more accurate way."

Where Kelly thinks that can go is the inclusion of expected goals as a featured stat. He understands that it's essentially a model and they can be harder to understand than real tangible information. But expected goals has a high correlation to winning a game, and best reflects the process of what's happening in the game.

"But from there, you can put it in more tangible terms," Kelly explains. "So slot shots is something that again, these are just shots that occur from that home plate area where 75 percent of goals are scored, correlates positively to winning or losing a hockey game. That's something that I think should be on these graphics and is available now and some of our partners actively do that."

INFORMATION AGE

In his role as an analyst for ESPN, Moore understands that it's his job to not only tell the viewer what is happening, but he also needs to explain why.

Analytics typically won't contradict a point he's trying to make, they will usually support it. He also realizes that some of the analytical information that is available can overwhelm even the most passionate of hockey fans.

"I'm analytically minded, and that's one of the reasons I really enjoy this role. So when I'm using data to help tell the story of the game, I need to make sure that what I'm delivering to the viewer will make sense within the context of that game," he explains.

"It's insightful to go deeper and try to pull something to provide more context. The data we have access to now is so much better than what we've had in the past, and that is a real asset to the viewer. But if what I'm saying is confusing the viewer, then I'm not doing my job."

THE PATH AHEAD

The NHL's puck and player tracking technology has already opened a lot of eyes with some of the data they've produced, but there's still room to improve.

There's going to be opportunity in a couple of areas in particular to take the next step with analytics and explore even further. Up until this point, there hasn't been a ton of work done in analytics to get more in-depth on player spacing on the ice, and to truly understand the impact of a defensive player.

For several years now, we have been able to look at the events that occur around the puck, and have a great understanding of the game and the way that it's played. Being able to explore the entire sheet of ice is where Kelly expects the next phase of analytics to grow.

"The next step beyond where I think we're heading towards is understanding what's happening away from the puck with as much granularity as possible. Being able to figure out where a player was on a back check, or how spread out the penalty kill unit was on a power play goal.

"It needs to be about understanding where players are that aren't directly involved in the play on the puck, and how that relates to the next play. This is something that we're going to be able to drill into a lot deeper. And just like everything we've been able to explore so far, I think there's a lot of really valuable insights that can come out of that."

FINAL WORDS

Any conversation about analytics always seems to involve a reference to the eye test. We are still in the early days of analytics in hockey though, so nothing is absolute.

Hockey is not baseball. Hockey is a very dynamic, fast moving, and complex sport. We've come a long way with analytics in a very short period of time, and there's still much to learn.

Hockey doesn't have the isolated one-on-one scenarios that exist in baseball. The acceptance and growth of analytics in baseball started much earlier, and they've invested a lot of time and resources into it. It's also easy to forget that there's so much more information to glean analytically from baseball.

It's for these reasons that Moore thinks we need to tread lightly and not jump to any conclusions with hockey analytics. As much as he enjoys digging into the numbers, Moore knows that any form of data can be misleading.

As we continue to move and grow with hockey analytics, it's important to have trained eyes on both sides of the equation. There will always be value in the eye test, but as analytics evolve, it's critically important to use the input and data available from each side of the aisle to get a broader perspective on analysis and decision-making.

"We really do need to still continue to take stock and account for the eye test, because experience counts for a lot in our game. It really does. And sometimes you'll still see and hear the experienced hockey people that are turned off by analytics, and they're not wrong. They have every right to feel that way.

"I really think it's just going to be a continual evolution. It's not to say that the numbers are always right, but that's not the truth either. I just think it's the wrong thing to discount, you know, things flat out like that. Because we know that data can lie too."

12

FUTURE OF HOCKEY

EXPANDED PLAYOFFS

The one hill that the NHL seems to want to die on is not changing the playoff format. Okay, that and the asinine situation in Arizona.

Their counterparts in the NBA already moved to include a play-in tournament, which gives some teams a last shot at making the postseason, and MLB expanded its playoffs last season.

But in listening to commissioner Gary Bettman in his press conference at the start of the 2022 Stanley Cup playoffs, it doesn't sound like it will be happening anytime soon:

"I think it creates great competition throughout the regular season, it makes the games most meaningful and there's nothing like our playoff tournament. The Stanley Cup is the hardest [championship] to win. And there's nothing in any sport like our first round."

The commish has a point. The first round of the NHL playoffs is some of the best theater in sports. But with so much emphasis put on divisional play, a few teams drew the short straw in 2022.

Hear me out on this. Nobody cares about the Atlantic, Metropolitan, Central, and Pacific divisions. Two words: Eastern and Western. Now that the league is at thirty-two teams with the addition of expansion Seattle in 2021–22, it's time to go back to the conference format that sends the top eight in each conference to the playoffs.

Let's take a look at how this would've shaped up in 2021–22, starting with the Eastern Conference.

Actual Divisional Format:

(A1) FLA vs (WC2) WSH, (M1) CAR vs (WC1) BOS, (A2) TOR vs (A3) TB, (M2) NYR vs (M3) PIT

But if we moved to a conference style, it would've shaken out like this:

(1)FLA vs (8) WSH, (2) CAR vs (7) PIT, (3) TOR vs (6) BOS, (4) NYR vs (5) TB

Three of the four series are completely different matchups. You can be sure that Toronto would've much preferred facing Boston over the defending Cup champs. It's also interesting to see that the eventual conference final matchup would've been a first round 4/5 tilt.

Now, let's give the Western Conference the same treatment.

Actual Divisional Format:

(C1) COL vs (WC2) NSH, (P1) CGY vs (WC1) DAL, (C2) MIN vs (C3) STL, (P1) EDM vs (P2) LA

Now, how the Western matchups would look in a top eight conference format:

(1)COL vs (8) NSH, (2) MIN vs (7) DAL, (3) CGY vs (6) LA, (4) STL vs (5) EDM

Incentivizing first place works again with the 1/8 series, but the other three look nothing the same. The biggest takeaway here is Minnesota would've avoided St. Louis in the first round, a series the Wild eventually lost four games to two. There should never be a scenario where two teams in the top four face each other in round one.

PLAY-IN TOURNAMENT

If you thought I was stopping at just blowing up the divisional format, buckle up for the NHL's new play-in tournament. This has a made-for-TV format written all over it, and I can't believe the league and their television partners aren't falling all over each other to make this happen.

Except for some last-minute tinkering in the East, and some subtle moves in the West, both conferences were essentially locked into their final eight playoff teams by December 1 of last season. It would've been nice to have some actual late-season drama to look forward to.

First off, the regular season has to end no later than a Thursday. This will give the teams competing in the tournament a couple of days to prepare, and it also adds some bonus downtime for the top six teams before they open up play.

The tournament will feature teams seven through ten from each conference. Just like in the NBA, seven plays eight, and nine faces ten. The winner of seven versus eight is automatically awarded the seventh spot in the postseason. The loser of seven versus eight then plays the winner of nine versus ten to get the eighth seed.

If the NFL can take over a weekend with their playoffs, so could the NHL. The Eastern Conference could play its two games in a Saturday doubleheader at four o'clock and eight o'clock, and the Western Conference will square off in the same timeslots on Sunday.

The games to decide the eighth and final spot in each conference would be played in prime time on Monday (East) and Tuesday (West). This plan's got television ratings gold written all over it.

If the play-in tournament had existed in 2022, the matchups would been as follows:

(7)Pittsburgh vs. (8) Washington; (9) NY Islanders vs. (10) Columbus

The Penguins-Capitals playoff rivalry has been epic over the years. This would've been a very juicy contest to look forward to.

And over in the West:

(7)Dallas vs (8) Nashville; (9) Vegas vs (10) Vancouver

Vancouver ended the year with six wins in their last 10 games, so you never know what kind of damage they might have done given a couple of extra shots at the postseason.

Make this happen, Mr. Bettman. Now.

YOUTH GONE WILD

It's all about skill and will, as the younger stars continue to drive the NHL. And if 2021–22 was any indication, I wouldn't expect this to slow down anytime soon.

In 2021–22, nine of the top ten scorers were under the age of 30, with 30-year-old Artemi Panarin serving as the elder statesman of the group. Five players were under 25, three were 28, and one was 26.

Of the seventeen players that reached the 40-goal mark, thirteen of them were under 30, and eight were 25 and younger. The baby of the group was Dallas' Jason Robertson, who scored 41 goals at the ripe old age of 22.

Go back ten years, and there were only four players who scored 40 goals during the 2011–12 season: Steven Stamkos (60), Evgeni Malkin (50), Marian Gaborik (41), and "The Real Deal" James Neal (40).

And if you're wondering which way the game is trending in terms of fighting, only thirteen players surpassed 100 minutes in penalties. Mark Borowiecki of Nashville was the leader of the goon squad with 151.

As a comparison, there were thirty-two players over 100 minutes a decade ago in 2011–12, led by the only 200-minute men in Derek Dorsett (235) and Zac Rinaldo (232).

GLOBAL GAME

The growth of the NHL as a truly global league continued in 2021–22, with players from eighteen different countries dotting the rosters of the thirty-two teams.

Canada leads the way with 484, followed by the United States (318), Sweden (106), and Russia 57).

Of the eighteen countries, four of them were represented by a single player: Australia (Nathan Walker), Netherlands (Daniel Sprong), Norway (Mats Zuccarello), and Slovenia (Anze Kopitar).

When Arizona native Auston Matthews took home the Hart Trophy as league MVP, he was one of four different players from four different nations to win a major award in 2021–22. Igor Shesterkin (Russia) won the Vezina Trophy, Moritz Seider (Germany) captured the Calder Trophy, and Cale Makar (Canada) claimed the Norris Trophy.

At the 2022 NHL Draft in Montreal, a total of 225 players were drafted from thirteen different countries. Canada topped the list with eighty-seven, and were joined by the United States (forty-nine), Sweden (twenty-six), Russia (twenty-five), and Finland (fourteen). Poland and Belarus each had one player selected.

There was also another milestone at the 2022 draft when Juraj Slafkovsky (Montreal) and Simon Nemec (New Jersey) became the first Slovakian players taken with the top two picks in the draft.

REALITY CHECK

There's more to hockey than how hard you can shoot or how fast you can skate. Bob Tetiva knew that being able to train your brain to process decision-making on the ice is as important a skill as skating or shooting, and that's why he developed Sense Arena in 2017.

The subscription-based virtual reality hockey simulator offers more than eighty different drills for players at all levels, from youth to professional. Using real-game scenarios, users are immersed into situations they are used to in live-game action by way of a VR headset.

To get started with Sense Arena, you'll need an Oculus Quest 2 VR headset with controllers, along with a haptic stick mount that will be attached to the stick just below the handle. While pressed against the stick's shaft, the controller will be able to accurately track all the user's movements while competing in the VR simulator. Goalies will require two controllers, with one strapped to both their catcher and blocker.

Sense Arena licenses start at forty-nine dollars per month depending on the number of users, and all data is stored in the cloud platform, including scores that are automatically downloaded after each drill is completed.

Based in Prague, Czech Republic, Sense Arena made its North American debut in 2019. The goalie program was introduced using Oculus in July 2020, with the player version following in July 2021. They already have more than nine thousand users in over thirty-three different countries including 120 professional organizations, and they are the official cognitive training tool of Arizona, Los Angeles, and New Jersey. The Vegas Golden Knights have also been using the system to help improve fan engagement at their practice facility.

Sense Arena isn't intended to replace practicing. The ultimate goal is to develop cognitive skills, fine-tune reaction time, quicken the reflexes, stimulate your senses, and strengthen overall play tracking. It's all about fine-tuning the skills of a player in all areas in a low-impact, high-intensity setting.

"It's really just about building a better athlete from the top down. The important part of how you impact the brain at a base level is through repetitions. We're not trying to install systems into the kids, and we're not trying to be the solution to teach you how to play hockey," says Tyler Lopinsky, Sense Arena's director of operations for North America. "What we can do is we can simulate a scenario over and over and over again. But not so that you remember the scenario. It's so you can learn it, download the information, and help create a solution as quickly as possible."

Users will take a baseline diagnostic test to determine their skill level and areas for development. Skaters are evaluated based on object tracking, looking for open lanes, reaction time, and peripheral vision. For goalies, it's about angles, puck tracking, play tracking, and save expectancy. An algorithm in the program then takes the results of the baseline test to create a training plan for the user to target specific areas of improvement.

In some cases, users can watch a 3D replay of the drill to see just how their actions played out. Goaltenders can view instant replays for all of their drills, and skaters have access to replays of the more complex ones. The goal of the replay is to not just to see how well you performed, but to spot any mistakes and areas of improvement that can be worked on.

And as the game evolves, so will Sense Arena. New drills will be added regularly based on input from their advisory board, including director of player development Andrew Alberts, a veteran of nine NHL seasons with Boston, Philadelphia, and Vancouver. Former NHL goaltending coach Brian Daccord serves as Sense Arena's director of goaltending development.

CUTTING EDGE

The NHL has been doing everything possible to reach the Gen Z market, and they've turned to virtual reality to make it happen.

If this generation is going to be staring at their phones while they're at a live game, they might as well be watching more hockey while they do it. In April 2022, the league rolled out NHL Edge, a real-time and immersive virtual reality program that works in conjunction with the league's puck and player tracking technology.

In an interview with ESPN's Greg Wyshynski at the launch event in New Jersey, Dave Lehanski, the NHL's executive vice president of business development and innovation, explained some of the rationale behind NHL Edge.

"How do we create an additive experience for kids at the game? What we want to do is take this experience and add stuff that people never contemplated before," Lehanski said. "There's the in-arena experience, and what we can do to enhance that technology. There's live-game presentation for everywhere outside of the building, like on your streaming application. And then there's like the really crazy stuff."

Real-time stats and information can be gleaned from the tracking data and streamed right to a user's iPhone while pointed at the ice while at a game. Player skating speed, shot attempts, faceoff stats—it will all be available as the action happens. Video highlights will also be added and updated throughout the game.

There's also the option of using VR devices like an Oculus headset to view the game live from a multitude of game angles using player perspectives.

The "really crazy stuff" that Lehanski mentions comes in the form of a real-time digital recreation of a game in 2-D using players in the blocky "Roblox" characters. The NFL streamed an entire wild-card playoff game using this technology from Beyond Sports, so you can be sure the NHL is already looking to enter the metaverse in the very near future.

GAME CHANGER

When expansion Seattle became the NHL's thirty-second franchise in 2021–22, they wanted to be more than just the new kid in town. For Kraken ownership, it was about growing the game of hockey in Seattle and leaving a lasting legacy for generations to come. That's where Climate Pledge Arena fits in.

Constructed on the site of the old Key Arena in downtown Seattle, Climate Pledge Arena was one of two new NHL buildings to open their doors in 2021, joining UBS Arena in Elmont, New York, home to the New York Islanders.

A unique project in many ways, Climate Pledge Arena uses the same iconic roof from Key Arena that made its debut during the 1962 World's Fair. The seating bowl was excavated nearly sixty feet below ground level, and the interior is bathed in natural light from some of the floor-to-ceiling windows of the building's exterior walls.

Even though Amazon purchased the naming rights in 2020, president Jeff Bezos decided to call it Climate Pledge Arena to help bring attention to the growing global climate crisis. But it's more than just a name. Climate Pledge Arena has truly lived up to its commitment to being a carbon-neutral sustainable facility.

They've eliminated the use for any fossil fuel throughout the building by using nothing but electricity to run everything from the mechanical systems and dehumidification tools, to all of the appliances used for cooking.

Seattle averages 150 days of rain per year, so it's only natural they've used that weather forecast to their advantage. The "Rain to Rink" system collects water that runs off the building's roof and accumulates in a fifteen-thousand-gallon cistern, a tank used for storing water that will be distributed afterwards. From there, the water is used in the ice-making process, making what the arena calls "the greenest ice in the NHL."

"I think it's a benchmark project that's going to be an influence on virtually everything that comes behind it. There's no question that our planet is in crisis. I think everybody knows that, but not everybody wants to acknowledge it," says Brad Clark from Populous, the architecture firm responsible for designing Climate Pledge Arena.

"I think Seattle is almost like a case study. We're going to be designing more sustainably, hiring more experts for our staff that are going to be tracking those efforts on every project we do. It's just the way of the future and I'm excited about it. In some ways it opens up a new frontier and puts us on a more civic-minded path to do our part."

While this all might sound ambitious and somewhat proprietary to a region like the Pacific Northwest, Clark believes there's no reason these features can't be incorporated into any future arena project in North America.

"You can build highly sustainable buildings in almost any location. It's always going to be driven by clients and their wallet, especially on privately funded projects. But I think we've proven that sustainable design and those metrics isn't all that more expensive to do than non-sustainable design if it's done the right way. We're always going to be at the mercy of our clients and what their expectations are, or what their desires are to go there. But we'll always be pushing them to the degree that we can."

MOVING FORWARD

As design firms and sports teams work together to create future arena and stadium projects, Scott Ralston of HOK says there needs to be a three-pronged approach included with each plan:

1. Create a microgrid

MicrogridKnowledge.com defines a microgrid as a self-sufficient energy system that serves a discrete geographic footprint, such as a college campus, hospital complex, business center, or neighborhood.

For a community that wants to become energy independent and environmentally friendly, Ralston says these are the perfect solution with new builds.

"We need to optimize a generation and the use of energy through the creation of microgrids with our future projects. That's not only going to be associated with arenas. In time, that'll be associated with hospitals, government buildings, everything.

"Arenas are one of those things that are so impactful and generational in nature in each city; you only get an arena every one or two generations. You don't get them often. They're the type of building that can be a pivot point in the life of a city because it draws just so much attention."

2. Sustainable facilities

Ralston shared that HOK has an arena design on the books that they are hoping to get built one day, and says it's even more sustainable than Climate Pledge Arena in a lot of respects. In his opinion, this should just be the tip of the iceberg.

"We need to be mindful of the total embodied carbon in these projects we are creating. How much carbon does it take, and so what does that mean? For one thing, concrete is terrible. Concrete is so awful with respect to carbon neutrality. So we need to figure out a way to get away from using concrete.

"We're actually exploring timber buildings. They've been done before, but the industry got away from it. But now with this pressure on, and being mindful of total embodied carbon, we have to allow ourselves to get away from concrete. We have to come up with strategies that deal with that. And so, we are beginning to look towards timber. It's not like you just drop a tree and you use a tree. There's things involved in it that make it safe. From day one when you start construction, through fifty years of operations, we want to take in the total carbon load. And there are ways to reduce the total carbon load in these buildings.

"Our clients, especially the cities, are now creating these policies towards carbon neutrality. Basically, whether they're knowingly doing this or not, they're asking us to design to carbon neutrality. And so our industry is heavily invested in that."

3. Community presence

Similar to how Little Caesars Arena has become an anchor point for several restaurants and businesses in the Detroit District, Ralston expects this to become the norm for arena and stadium projects in cities around the world.

"We see these buildings continuing to become more and more extroverted. Meaning, they're going to continue to open up more to the community and become more of a day-to-day community asset with things embedded that support the surrounding community. Even something as basic as commercial and spaces. Ideally, they'll be enriching the lives of people that may not necessarily ever go to a ticketed event, and just become a little bit more integrated in that community.

ABOUT THE AUTHOR & ACKNOWLEDGMENTS

Kevin Snow has an extensive professional background in sports and media in both the United States and Canada, and his work has been published across North America for various print and digital outlets. He has written three books and also spent ten years with the NHL's Buffalo Sabres in public relations and content management. He resides in Buffalo, New York.

Special thanks to everyone at Skyhorse Publishing, especially the very patient Julie Ganz.

My heartfelt thanks goes out to the following individuals for taking the time to speak with me for this project: Dave Barr, Mike Bracko, Brad Clark, Sam Cosentino, John Davidson, Rob Day, Anthony Fisher, Roch Gaudreau, Chris Gear, Bob Gehrz, Alain Hache, Mike Kelly, Tyler Lopinsky, Patrick Love, Bill McCarthy, Lisa McDowell, Matt Messer, Dominic Moore, Chris Nowinski, Scott Ralston, Gary Roberts, Jeff Serowik, Tyson Teplitsky, Tim Turk, John Vogl, and Kevin Woodley. Not to mention all the public relations and marketing people that helped coordinate all of the interviews.

And a special thanks to my friend and former podcast pal Kevin Sylvester for making this happen in the first place.